By Shane Hensley, Paul "Wiggy" Wade-Williams, Simon Lucas, Joseph Unger, Dave Blewer, Clint Black, Robin Elliott, Piotr Koryś

With "Evil" Mike, "Chaos" Steve, Zeke Sparkes, Jay & Amy Kyle, Jodi Black, Dirk Ringersma, Randy Mosiondz

Special thanks to Kirsty Lucas, Michelle, Caden, and Ronan Hensley, Cecil & Sheila Hensley, Jackie Unger, Maggie Wade-Williams, Justyna Koryś

Additional thanks to the 12 to Midnight crew, Andy Hopp, Legion, Sean-Patrick Fannon, & Sean Preston

Special Thanks to Frank Uchmanowicz and Jim Searcy of Studio2.

Cover and Graphics by Cheyenne Wright

Interior Illustrations: Cheyenne Wright, Ron Spencer, Brian Snoddy, Todd Lockwood, Max Humber, Pawel Klopotowski, Chris Waller, Storn, Gil Formosa, Talisman Studios, Daniel Rudnicki, Slawomir Maniak, Chris Malidore, Leanne Buckley, Julie Dillon, Nicole Cardiff, Christophe Swal, Satya Hody, Niklas Brandt, Aaron Acevedo, Chris Griffin, Vincent Hie, Christophe Swal, John Worsley, Courtesy of Empty Room Studios: Mike Hamlett, Dan Howard, and Joe Slucher

Dedicated to all those who have helped and volunteered to make Savage Worlds such a success

Also dedicated to the new little Savage, Dylan Michael Lucas.

Savage Worlds Explorer's Edition 2nd Printing

CONTENTS

Game Master's Section

Savage Worlds!

Welcome to *Savage Worlds*—a merger of the best ideas in roleplaying and miniature battles!

Savage Worlds was designed to be easy for the Game Master to write adventures, create new villains and monsters, track NPCs in combat, and run epic tales, while still giving players all the character development and advancement they're used to from more system-heavy games.

Because combat requires little bookkeeping, you can fight out your heroes' most epic battles to save the world right on the table-top with *dozens* of allies and foes!

Finally, *Savage Worlds* was designed to be used with any genre—from swashbuckling pirates to superheroes and sci-fi. It's easy to create your own world or play in one of our Savage Settings (information on our current settings can be found at the end of this book).

There's lots more to tell you about, so let's get to it!

Getting Started

Here's what you need to get started!

Dice

Savage Worlds uses all 6 traditional gaming dice: 4-sided, 6-sided, 8-sided, 10-sided, 12-sided, and occasionally 20-sided dice. All of these are available from your favorite local gaming store, or online directly from Pinnacle.

Like most roleplaying games, we abbreviate the different dice as d4, d6, d8, d10, d12, and d20. If you see something like 2d6, that means to roll two six-sided dice and add them up.

Players need only one set of these dice. The Game Master might want a couple of sets so she can roll attacks for several villains at once.

Cards

Savage Worlds uses a standard deck of playing cards with the Jokers left in. Cards are used for initiative in combat and to help keep things moving fast and furious. You'll even find an official set of *Savage Worlds* oversized cards where you found this book!

A Setting

Will you and your friends explore post-apocalyptic ruins? Lead a rugged warband in your favorite fantasy world? Take on the role of vampire lords? Or perhaps fight evil in the many theatres of *Weird Wars?*

Pick up the book for your favorite game setting at your local game store, or create your own. Official Savage Settings include new Edges and Hindrances, Setting Rules, spells, weapons, gear, monsters, and more!

Figures and Battle Mats

Figures of some sort are very useful for running *Savage Worlds* games. Metal miniatures are available from several manufacturers, and cheaper full-color cardstock heroes and monsters can be found as well. In these rules, we assume you're using 28mm figures—the standard "large size" hobby gaming miniature. Ranges for weapons, movement, and everything else is figured for this size figure on the table-top. If you're using larger or smaller figures, you may want to adjust your ranges to make things look a little more realistic.

It's essential to have some kind of gaming surface as well, either a terrain board or a Chessex Battle Mat™. We recommend the latter. That way the GM can draw out the tactical situation with water-soluble markers so that everyone can see what's going on and make the most of their surroundings. Mapping out a battle can really help everyone understand where their characters are, where their allies are, and what terrain features they might be able to make use of for cover or clever tricks and maneuvers.

CHAPTER ONE: CHARACTER CREATION

Creating awesome heroes couldn't be easier. The only thing you need is a copy of the character sheet found at our website WWW.PEGINC.COM. This section assumes you're starting as a "Novice." We'll explain what that means in more detail later in this book.

1) RACE

Humans are the most common characters, but some Savage Settings may feature bizarre aliens, graceful elves, or other exotic races. You can choose to play any race available in your particular setting.

Humans are the standard race in *Savage Worlds,* and start play with one free Edge (see Step 3).

2) TRAITS

Characters are defined by attributes and skills, collectively called "Traits," and both work in exactly the same way. Attributes and skills are ranked by die types, from a d4 to a d12, with d6 being the average for adult humans. Higher is better!

ATTRIBUTES

Every character starts with a d4 in each attribute, and has 5 points with which to raise them. Raising a d4 to a d6, for example, costs 1 point. You're free to spend these points however you want with one exception: no attribute may be raised above a d12.

• **Agility** is your hero's nimbleness, quickness, and dexterity.
• **Smarts** is a measure of how well your character knows his world and culture, how well he thinks on his feet, and mental agility.

• **Spirit** reflects inner wisdom and willpower. Spirit is very important as it helps your character recover from being rattled when injured.
• **Strength** is raw physical power and general fitness. Strength is also used to generate your warrior's damage in hand-to-hand combat.
• **Vigor** represents endurance, resistance to disease, poison, or toxins, and how much pain and physical damage a hero can shake off.

SKILLS

Skills are learned trades such as Shooting, Fighting, scientific knowledge, professional abilities, and so on. These are very general descriptions which cover all related aspects. Shooting, for example, covers all types of guns, bows, rocket launchers, and other ranged weapons.

You have 15 points to distribute among your skills. Each die type costs 1 point as long as the skill is equal to or less than the attribute it's linked to (listed beside the skill in parentheses). If you exceed the attribute, the cost becomes 2 points per die type.

As with attributes, no skill may be increased above d12.

Example: Fighting is linked to Agility. A character with a d8 Agility can buy Fighting for one point per die type to d8. Buying a d10 costs 2 points, and a d12 costs another 2 points.

DERIVED STATISTICS

Your character sheet contains a few other statistics you need to fill in, described below.

Pace is how fast your character moves in a standard combat round. Humans walk 6" in a round and can move an additional 1d6" if they run. Write "6" on your character sheet beside the word Pace. This is 6" on the table-top—every inch there represents 2 yards in the "real world."

Parry is equal to 2 plus half your character's Fighting (2 if a character does not have Fighting), plus any bonuses for shields or certain weapons. This is the TN to hit your hero in hand-to-hand combat.

For stats such as d12+1, add half the fixed modifier, rounded down. For instance, a Fighting skill of d12+1 grants a Parry of 8, whereas a d12+2 gives a Parry of 9.

Charisma is a measure of your character's appearance, manner, and general likability. It's 0 unless you have Edges or Hindrances that modify it. Charisma is added to Persuasion and Streetwise rolls, and is used by the GM to figure out how nonplayer characters react to your hero.

Toughness is your hero's damage threshold. Anything over this causes him to be rattled or worse. Like Parry, Toughness is 2 plus half your hero's Vigor, plus Armor (use the armor worn on his torso). Vigor over a d12 is calculated just like Parry.

3) EDGES & HINDRANCES

Great heroes are far more than a collection of skills and attributes. It's their unique gifts, special powers, and tragic flaws that truly make them interesting characters.

Characters can take Edges by balancing them out with Hindrances. You'll find a complete list of Edges and Hindrances in the next section. Look for more in upcoming Savage Settings.

You can take one Major Hindrance and two Minor Hindrances. A Major Hindrance is worth 2 points, and a Minor Hindrance is worth 1 point.

For 2 points you can:
• Raise an attribute one die type (you may raise your attributes before purchasing skills).
• Choose an Edge.

For 1 point you can:
• Gain another skill point.
• Gain additional money equal to your starting funds (if you start with $500, you gain an additional $500)

4) GEAR

Next you need to purchase equipment. Some settings may provide your hero with all the gear he needs. In others, you may be assigned a certain amount of money with which to purchase your starting gear. A list of some common gear and weapons can be found in Chapter Two.

Unless your setting book or GM says otherwise, the standard starting amount is $500.

5) BACKGROUND DETAILS

Finish your character by filling in any history or background you care to. Ask yourself why your hero is where she is and what her goals are. Or you can just start playing and fill in these details as they become important.

SKILLS

Below are skills available in most Savage Settings. These skills are very generic—you don't need five different Shooting skills to shoot pistols, rifles, machine-guns, bows, and rocket launchers. Nor do you need different Driving skills for every common vehicle in your setting. We've made the skills as simple and comprehensive as possible so that you can get on with the game instead of keeping track of a shopping list of skills.

Boating (Agility)

Characters with this skill can handle most any boat common to their setting. They generally know how to handle most common tasks associated with their vessels as well (tying knots, simple engine repair, etc).

Rules for using boats on the table-top can be found in Chapter Five.

Climbing (Strength)

This is the skill characters use to ascend walls, trees, or cliff-sides. No roll is usually needed to ascend ladders, ropes, or trees with lots of limbs unless the GM feels there's a good reason (being chased, wounded, etc).

Those who have high Climbing skill are those who frequently climb cliffs, walls, and other difficult surfaces.

Characters about to ascend a difficult surface must make a Climbing roll every 10" (20 yards). The skill roll is modified by the conditions below.

During combat, characters ascend at half their Strength per round if using ropes or with decent hand- or footholds.

See the Falling rules should a character suffer a mishap.

Climbing Modifiers

Situation	Modifier
Climbing equipment	+2
Advanced climbing equipment	+4
Scarce or thin handholds	−2
Wet surface	−2

Driving (Agility)

Driving allows your hero to drive ground and hover vehicles common to his setting. You'll find complete rules for driving everything from motorcycles to hovertanks in Chapter Five.

Fighting (Agility)

Fighting covers all hand-to-hand (melee) attacks. The TN to hit an opponent is his Parry (2 plus half his Fighting).

Gambling (Smarts)

Gambling is useful in many settings, from the saloons of the Old West to the barracks of most armies. Here's a quick way to simulate about a half-hour of gambling without having to roll for every single toss of the dice or hand of cards.

First have everyone agree on the stakes. Five dollars, 5 gold coins, etc., is recommended for a typical game. Now have everyone in the game make a Gambling roll. The lowest total pays the highest total the difference times the stake. The next lowest pays the second highest the difference times the stake, and so on. If there's an odd man left in the middle, he breaks even.

Cheating: A character who cheats adds +2 to his roll. The GM may raise or lower this modifier depending on the particulars of the game or the method of cheating. If the player ever rolls a 1 on his skill die (regardless of his Wild Die), he's caught. The consequences of this depend on the setting, but are usually quite harsh.

GUTS (SPIRIT)

Guts reflects a hero's bravery. Characters are often called on to make Guts checks when they witness grisly scenes or encounter particularly horrific monsters. The GM should see the **Fear** table for the effects of failure.

HEALING (SMARTS)

Healing is the art of stopping wounds and treating existing injuries. See the Healing rules for specific information.

INTIMIDATION (SPIRIT)

Intimidation is the art of frightening an opponent with sheer force of will, veiled or overt threats, or sometimes just really big guns. This is an opposed roll between the hero's Intimidation and his opponent's Spirit. See Tests of Will for the game effects.

INVESTIGATION (SMARTS)

A character skilled in Investigation knows how to make good use of libraries, newspaper morgues, the internet, or other written sources of information. To get information from people rather than books and computers, use the Streetwise skill.

KNOWLEDGE (SMARTS)

Knowledge is a catch-all skill that must have a focus of some sort, such as Knowledge (Occult) or Knowledge (Science). The player can choose the focus of his character's knowledge, which should reflect his background and education. An archaeologist, for example, should have Knowledge (History) and Knowledge (Archaeology). The skill can be taken multiple times with different focuses to reflect different areas of expertise.

General focuses such as Science are acceptable, but the GM should give a bonus to a character who has a more relevant focus, such as Knowledge (Biology).

Some suggested Knowledge focuses are: Area Knowledge, Battle (used in Mass Combats), Computers, Electronics, History, Journalism, various languages, Law, Medicine (though actually caring for someone is the Healing skill), Science, or Tactics.

LOCKPICKING (AGILITY)

Lockpicking is the ability to bypass mechanical and electronic locks. Lockpicking is also be used to disarm the catches and triggers on traps, unless a more relevant skill seems appropriate for a particular trap.

NOTICE (SMARTS)

Notice is a hero's general alertness and ability to search for items or clues. This covers hearing rolls, detecting ambushes, spotting hidden weapons and even scrutinizing other characters to see if they're lying, frightened, and so on.

PERSUASION (SPIRIT)

Persuasion is the ability to talk or trick others into doing what you want. Nonplayer characters start at one of five different attitudes: Hostile, Uncooperative, Neutral, Friendly, or Helpful. A successful Persuasion roll improves the NPC's attitude one step, or two with a raise. Failure, on the other hand, decreases the character's attitude by a step, or two if a 1 is rolled on the Persuasion die (regardless of the Wild Die).

Persuasion is always modified by a character's Charisma. The GM has more detailed information on nonplayer characters and their reactions.

PILOTING (AGILITY)

Piloting allows a character to fly airplanes, helicopters, jet packs, and any other flying devices common to his setting.

REPAIR (SMARTS)

Repair is the ability to fix gadgets, vehicles, weapons, and other machines. Characters suffer a −2 penalty to their rolls if they don't have access to basic tools.

RIDING (AGILITY)

Riding allows you to mount, control, and ride any beast common to your setting. Players should note that mounted characters use the lowest of their Fighting or Riding skills when fighting from horseback.

SHOOTING (AGILITY)

Shooting covers all attempts to hit a target with a ranged weapon such as a bow, pistol, or rocket launcher. The basic Target Number to hit is 4 as usual, though there are a number of important modifiers such as range that frequently come into play.

STEALTH (AGILITY)

Stealth is the ability to both hide and move quietly, as well as palm objects and pick pockets. In many *Savage Worlds* games, knowing exactly when your hero has been spotted and when he's not can be critical.

Here are detailed rules for how to sneak up on foes and infiltrate enemy lines. Start by figuring out if the "guards" your heroes are sneaking up on are "active" or "inactive."

Inactive guards aren't paying particularly close attention to their surroundings. The group need only score a standard success on their individual Stealth rolls to avoid being seen. Failing a Stealth roll in the presence of inactive guards makes them active.

COMMON KNOWLEDGE

Instead of forcing characters to have dozens of "background" skills they rarely need, we use the concept of "Common Knowledge." Your hero knows the basic history of his land, common etiquette, how to get around geographically, and who the major players in his locality are. This is called "Common Knowledge," and is covered by your hero's Smarts attribute.

If a character's background suggests he should know something about a subject, add +2 or more to his roll. If the subject is foreign to a character, subtract 2 or more from the roll. Everyone else breaks even and gets no modifier.

Anytime an adventure asks for a Common Knowledge roll, the GM should ask for Smarts rolls and subjectively and on the fly grant bonuses or subtract penalties to account for each character's particular background.

Here's an example. Let's say an adventure reads: "Anyone who makes a Common Knowledge roll detects that this cavern was carved by civilized hands, not formed naturally." A dwarf knows more about stonework than an elf, so give the dwarf a +2 to his roll. A human has about average knowledge, so no bonus is granted. An elf, who has spent most of his life in a tree, won't be able to tell unless there are obvious signs, and so gets a –2.

If it becomes important to know how well a character *performs* a common task, the GM can ask for whatever roll is appropriate. Knowing how to do a dance, for example, is a Common Knowledge roll. If it becomes important to see how well a character performs the dance, the GM might ask for an Agility roll (with no bonuses or penalties).

SPECIFIC KNOWLEDGES

Sometimes a character might want more detailed or specific knowledge. This is encouraged and adds a whole new level of expertise to the character's information. In the example above, a dwarf with Knowledge (Stonework) not only knows the dungeon was carved, but might just know what race did it, and the era in which it was carved.

Knowledge of a particular region is also handy. In a fantasy campaign, for example, locals might know the Dread Mountains are home to vicious harpies. Someone with a specific knowledge of that area can make a roll to see if he knows a safe route through the mountains, or the specific peak the creatures' aerie is in.

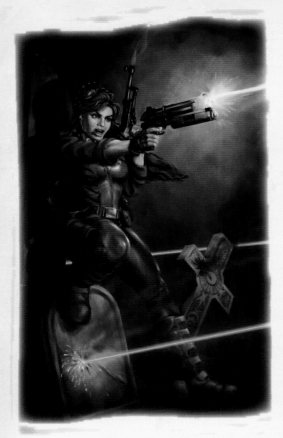

The Last Step: Sneaking to within 5" of a foe (usually to get close enough for a melee attack) requires an opposed Stealth roll versus the target's Notice, whether the guard is active or inactive.

Movement Rate: Outside of combat, each Stealth roll covers moving up to five times the character's Pace. In combat, the Stealth roll covers only a single round of movement.

Stealth for Groups: Out of combat, make only one Stealth roll for each like group of characters (a group roll). Use the lowest movement rate to determine how much ground is covered as well. The observers also make a group roll to Notice their foes.

Once a combat breaks down into rounds, Stealth and Notice rolls are made on an individual basis.

Streetwise (Smarts)

Streetwise characters are able to gather information from the street, saloons, or other contacts through bribes, threats, or carousing. Finding written information in libraries and the like is covered by the Investigation skill.

Streetwise is always modified by a character's Charisma modifier.

Survival (Smarts)

Survival allows a character to find food, water, or shelter in hostile environments. A character may only make one roll per day. A successful roll finds sustenance for one person, a raise on the roll finds food and water for five adults. Horses and other large beasts count as two adults. Children, camels or others with small appetites count as half. Those who benefit from the roll do not have to make Fatigue rolls for the day for food, water, or shelter.

Swimming (Agility)

Swimming determines if a character floats or sinks in water, as well as how fast he can move within it. A character's Pace is half his Swimming skill in inches per turn in normal water (round up). Choppy water counts as

Active guards make opposed Notice rolls against the sneaking characters' Stealth skills. Failing a roll against active guards means the sneaking character is spotted.

Apply the following modifiers to all Stealth rolls.

Stealth Modifiers

Situation	Modifier
Crawling	+2
Running	–2
Dim light	+1
Darkness	+2
Pitch darkness	+4
Light cover	+1
Medium cover	+2
Heavy cover	+4

rough terrain and halves this rate. Characters may not "run" while swimming for extra movement.

Should it become important, characters can hold their breath for 5 x their Vigor in seconds, or half that if they weren't prepared.

Taunt (Smarts)

Taunt is a test of will attack against a person's pride through ridicule, cruel jokes, or one-upmanship. This is an opposed roll against the target's Smarts. See Test of Wills for the effects of a successful Taunt.

Throwing (Agility)

Throwing governs all sorts of thrown weapons, from hand grenades to knives, axes, and spears.

Throwing works just like the Shooting skill, and uses all the same modifiers.

Tracking (Smarts)

Tracking allows a character to follow the tracks of one or more individuals in any type of terrain.

Each roll generally covers following the tracks for one mile, but the GM may adjust this dramatically for more specific or small scale searches.

Apply the modifiers below to each roll.

Tracking Modifiers

Situation	Modifier
Tracking more than 5 individuals	+2
Recent snow	+4
Mud	+2
Dusty area	+1
Raining	–4
Tracking in poor light	–2
Tracks are more than one day old	–2
Target attempted to hide tracks	–2

HINDRANCES

Hindrances are character flaws and physical handicaps that occasionally make life a little tougher for your hero. Some Hindrances are more or less subjective (such as Overconfident). They're there to help you roleplay your character, and might even net you more bennies!

A character may take one Major Hindrance and up to two Minor Hindrances. You're free to take more if you think they fit your character description, but you don't get additional points for them.

ALL THUMBS (MINOR)

Some people just aren't good with modern devices. Characters with this drawback suffer a –2 penalty to the Repair skill at all times. In addition, when a hero uses a mechanical or electronic device, a roll of 1 on his skill die (regardless of his Wild Die) means the device is broken. The damage usually requires a Repair roll at –2 and 1d6 hours to fix.

ANEMIC (MINOR)

Your hero is particularly susceptible to sickness, disease, environmental effects, and fatigue. He subtracts 2 from all Vigor rolls made to resist Fatigue checks, poison, disease, and the like.

ARROGANT (MAJOR)

Your hero doesn't think he's the best—he knows he is. Whatever it is—swordsmanship, kung fu, running—there is no one who can touch his skills and he flaunts it every chance he gets.

Winning just isn't enough for your hero. He must completely dominate his opponent. Anytime there is even a shadow of a doubt as to who is the better, he must humiliate his opponent and prove he can snatch victory any time he wishes. He is the kind of man who disarms an opponent in a duel just so he can pick the sword up and hand it back with a smirk.

Arrogant heroes always look for the "master" in battle, attacking lesser minions only if they get in the way.

BAD EYES (MINOR OR MAJOR)

Your hero's eyes just aren't what they used to be. With glasses, there's no penalty and the Hindrance is only Minor. Should he lose his glasses (generally a 50% chance when he's wounded, or no chance with a "nerd-strap"), he suffers a –2 penalty to any Trait roll made to shoot or Notice something more than 5" (10 yards) distant.

In low-tech settings where the hero cannot wear glasses, Bad Eyes is a Major Hindrance. He must subtract 2 from Trait rolls made to attack or notice things 5" or more away.

BAD LUCK (MAJOR)

Your hero is a little less lucky than most. He gets one less benny per game session than normal. A character cannot have both Bad Luck and Good Luck.

Big Mouth (Minor)

Loose lips sink ships, the saying goes. Your hero's could drown an armada.

Your character can't keep a secret very well. He reveals plans and gives away things best kept among friends, usually at the worst possible times.

Blind (Major)

Your hero is completely without sight. He suffers a –6 to all physical tasks that require vision—which is most everything, and –2 to most social tasks as he can't "read" those he's interacting with as well as others.

On the plus side, Blind characters gain their choice of a free Edge to compensate for this particularly deadly Hindrance.

Bloodthirsty (Major)

Your hero never takes prisoners unless under the direct supervision of a superior. This can cause major problems in a military campaign unless your superiors condone that sort of thing. Your hero suffers –4 to his Charisma, but only if his cruel habits are known.

Cautious (Minor)

Some folks gather too much intelligence. This character personifies over-cautiousness. He never makes rash decisions and likes to plot things out in detail long before any action is taken.

Clueless (Major)

Your hero isn't as aware of his world as most others. He suffers –2 to Common Knowledge rolls.

Code of Honor (Major)

Honor is very important to your character. He keeps his word, won't abuse or kill prisoners, and generally tries to operate within his world's particular notion of proper gentlemanly or ladylike behavior.

Curious (Major)

It killed the cat, and it might kill your hero as well. Curious characters are easily dragged into any adventure. They have to check out everything and always want to know what's behind a potential mystery.

Death Wish (Minor)

Having a death wish doesn't mean your hero is suicidal—but he does want to die *after* completing some important goal. Maybe he wants revenge for the murder of his family, or maybe he's dying from disease and wants to go out in a blaze of glory. He won't throw his life away for no reason, but when there's a chance to complete his goal, he'll do anything—and take any risk—to achieve it.

This Hindrance is usually Minor unless the goal is relatively easily fulfilled (very rare).

Delusional (Minor or Major)

Your hero believes something that is considered quite strange by everyone else. Minor Delusions are harmless or the character generally keeps it to himself (the government puts sedatives in soft drinks, dogs can talk, we're all just characters in some bizarre game, etc).

With a Major Delusion, he expresses his view on the situation frequently and it can occasionally lead to danger (the government is run by aliens, hospitals are deadly, I'm allergic to armor, zombies are my friends).

Doubting Thomas (Minor)

Some people don't believe in the supernatural until they're halfway down some creature's gullet. Doubting Thomases are skeptics who try their best to rationalize supernatural events. Even once a Doubting Thomas realizes the supernatural exists, he still tries to rationalize weird events, following red herrings or ignoring evidence.

Doubting Thomases suffer –2 to their Guts checks when confronted with undeniable supernatural horror.

ELDERLY (MAJOR)

Your hero is getting on in years, but he's not quite ready for the nursing home. His Pace is reduced by 1, and his Strength and Vigor drop a die type to a minimum of d4, and cannot be raised thereafter.

On the plus side, the wisdom of his years grants the hero 5 extra skill points that may be used for any skills linked to Smarts.

ENEMY (MINOR OR MAJOR)

Someone out there hates your hero and wants him dead. The value of the Hindrance depends on how powerful the enemy is and how often he might show up. A Minor Enemy might be a lone gunslinger out for vengeance. A Major Enemy might be a supernatural gunslinger with a hate-on for your hero.

If the enemy is one day defeated, the GM should gradually work in a replacement, or the hero may buy off the Hindrance by sacrificing a leveling opportunity.

GREEDY (MINOR OR MAJOR)

Your miserly hero measures his worth in treasure. If a Minor Hindrance, he argues bitterly over any loot acquired during play. If a Major Hindrance, he fights over anything he considers unfair, and may even kill for his "fair share."

HABIT (MINOR OR MAJOR)

Your warrior has an annoying and constant habit of some sort. Maybe she picks her nose, says "y'know" in every sentence, or chews gum like it's going out of style.

A Minor Habit irritates those around her but isn't dangerous. Your hero suffers a –1 Charisma.

A Major Habit is a physical or mental addiction of some sort that is debilitating or possibly even deadly. This includes drug use, chronic drinking, or perhaps even an addiction to virtual reality in a high-tech setting. A character who doesn't get his fix must make a Fatigue check every 24 hours thereafter (see **Fatigue**). The first failed roll makes the character Fatigued, then Exhausted. The final result is a coma for hard drug use, or a bad case of the shakes for things like alcohol or VR. Medical care may ease the symptoms. Otherwise the victim must live with the penalties for 1d6 days. Afterwards, the hero must buy off the Hindrance by sacrificing an opportunity to level up, or he eventually falls back into his dependency.

HARD OF HEARING (MINOR OR MAJOR)

Characters who have lost some or all of their hearing have this disadvantage. As a Minor Hindrance, it subtracts 2 from all Notice rolls made to hear, including awaking due to loud noises. A Major Hindrance means the character is deaf. She cannot hear and automatically fails all Notice rolls that depend on hearing.

HEROIC (MAJOR)

Your hero never says no to a person in need. She doesn't have to be happy about it, but she always comes to the rescue of those she feels can't help themselves. She's the first one to run into a burning building, usually agrees to hunt monsters for little or no pay, and is generally a pushover for a sob story.

ILLITERATE (MINOR)

Your hero cannot read. He can probably sign his name and knows what a STOP sign says, but can do little else. He also doesn't know much about math either. He can probably do 2+2=4, but multiplication and the like are beyond him.

Illiterates can't read or write in any language, by the way, no matter how many they actually speak.

LAME (MAJOR)

A past wound has nearly crippled your hero. His basic Pace is reduced by 2 and he rolls only a d4 for running rolls. A character's Pace may never be reduced below 1.

LOYAL (MINOR)

Your character may not be a hero, but he'd give his life for his friends. This character can never leave a man behind if there's any chance at all he could help.

MEAN (MINOR)

Your hero is ill-tempered and disagreeable. No one really likes him, and he has trouble doing anything kind for anyone else. He must be paid for his troubles and doesn't even accept awards graciously. Your hero suffers −2 to his Charisma.

OBESE (MINOR)

Particularly large people often have great difficulty in dangerous physical situations. Those who carry their weight well have the Brawny Edge. Those who don't handle it very well are Obese. A character cannot be both Brawny and Obese.

An Obese hero adds 1 to his Toughness, but his Pace is decreased by 1 and his running die is a d4.

Obese characters may also have difficulty finding armor or clothing that fits, fitting into tight spaces, or even riding in confined spaces such as coach airplane seats or compact cars.

ONE ARM (MAJOR)

Whether by birth or battle, your hero has lost an arm. Fortunately, his other arm is (now) his "good" one. Tasks that require two hands, such as Climbing, suffer a −4 modifier.

ONE EYE (MAJOR)

Your hero has had an eye gouged out by some nefarious villain in his past. If he doesn't wear a patch or buy a glass replacement (typically $500), he suffers −1 to his Charisma for the grotesque wound.

He suffers −2 to any Trait rolls that require depth perception, such as Shooting or Throwing, jumping from one mast to another, and so on.

ONE LEG (MAJOR)

With a peg, One Leg acts exactly like the Lame Hindrance, reducing Pace by 2 and running rolls are now a d4. Without a peg, the character's Pace is 2 and he can never run. He also suffers −2 to Traits that require mobility, such as Climbing and Fighting.

A character with one leg also suffers a −2 penalty to his Swimming skill (and Pace).

OUTSIDER (MINOR)

In a society made up of only a few types of people, your hero isn't one of them. An Indian in a Western town, an alien in a sci-fi game of human marines, or an orc in a party of elves, dwarves, and humans are all examples of outsiders. These people are also likely to raise prices on the Outsider, ignore pleas for help, and generally treat him as if he's of a lower class than the rest of their society.

In addition to the roleplaying effects above, your hero's Charisma suffers a –2 modifier among all but his own people.

OVERCONFIDENT (MAJOR)

There's nothing out there your hero can't defeat. At least that's what he thinks. He believes he can do most anything and never wants to retreat from a challenge. He's not suicidal, but he certainly takes on more than common sense dictates.

PACIFIST (MINOR OR MAJOR)

Your hero absolutely despises violence. Minor pacifism means he only fights when given no other choice, and never allows the killing of prisoners or other defenseless victims.

Major Pacifists won't fight living characters under *any* circumstances. They may defend themselves, but won't do anything to permanently harm sentient, living creatures. Note that undeniably evil creatures, undead, demons and the like, are fair game, however. A Major Pacifist might also fight with nonlethal methods, such as with his fists. Such characters only do so when obviously threatened, however.

PHOBIA (MINOR OR MAJOR)

Phobias are overwhelming and irrational fears that stay with a hero for the rest of his life. Whenever a character is in the presence of his phobia, he subtracts 2 from all his Trait tests as a Minor Hindrance, and 4 if the fear is a Major Phobia.

Phobias shouldn't be too obvious— everyone should be afraid of vampires, for example, so it's not a phobia—it's common sense. Instead, the phobia usually centers on some random element the mind focused on during whatever encounter caused such a fright. Remember, phobias are *irrational* fears.

POVERTY (MINOR)

It's said a fool and his money are soon parted. Your hero is that fool. He starts with half the usual money for your setting and just can't seem to hang onto funds acquired after play. In general, the player should halve his total funds every game week or so.

QUIRK (MINOR)

Your hero has some minor foible that is usually humorous, but can occasionally cause him trouble. A swashbuckler may always try to first slash his initials on his foes before attacking, a dwarf may brag constantly about his culture, or a snobby debutante might not eat, drink, or socialize with the lower class.

SMALL (MAJOR)

Your character is either very skinny, very short, or both relative to his particular race. Subtract 1 from your hero's Toughness for his reduced stature.

STUBBORN (MINOR)

Your hero always wants his way and never admits he's wrong. Even when it's painfully obvious he's made a mistake, he tries to justify it with half-truths and rationalizations.

UGLY (MINOR)

Your hero hit more than a few ugly sticks on his way down the tree of life. His Charisma is lowered by 2, and he is generally shunned by members of the opposite sex.

VENGEFUL (MINOR OR MAJOR)

Your character always attempts to right a wrong he feels was done to him. If this is a Minor Hindrance, he usually seeks vengeance legally. If this is a Major Hindrance, he'll kill to see it done.

VOW (MINOR OR MAJOR)

The character has a vow of some sort. Whether it's Major or Minor depends on the Vow itself. Some may have Vows to particular orders or causes, to the Hippocratic Oath, to rid the world of evil, and so on. The danger in fulfilling the Vow and how often it might come into play determines the level of the Hindrance.

Whatever the Vow, it's only a Hindrance if it actually comes into play from time to time and causes the character some discomfort.

WANTED (MINOR OR MAJOR)

Your hero has committed some crime in his past and will be arrested if discovered by the authorities. This assumes the setting actually has laws and police officers to enforce them.

The level of the Hindrance depends on how serious the crime was. A hero with numerous unpaid parking tickets (in a game where he might have to drive occasionally) has a Minor Hindrance, as does someone wanted for more serious crimes away from the main campaign area. Being accused of murder is a Major Hindrance in almost any setting.

YELLOW (MAJOR)

Not everyone has ice water in his veins. Your hero is squeamish at the sight of blood and gore and terrified of coming to harm. He subtracts 2 from all of his Guts checks.

YOUNG (MAJOR)

Children are sometimes forced to go on dangerous adventures through unfortunate circumstances. Think carefully before choosing this Hindrance, for your character starts at a significant disadvantage.

Young heroes are generally 8-12 years old (in human years—you must adjust this for races with different aging paradigms). They have only 3 points to adjust their attributes and 10 skill points. On the plus side, youths like these have a fair amount of luck. They draw one extra benny at the beginning of each game session. This is in addition to any additional bennies gained from such things as the Luck or Great Luck Edges.

If the character should live long enough to mature, the Hindrance doesn't have to be bought off, he's already paid the price for the Hindrance by starting at a disadvantage. He stops getting the extra benny when he reaches 18 years of age however (or the age of adulthood in your particular setting).

19

EDGES

Below is a list of Edges common to most settings. You'll find more Edges in official *Savage Worlds* setting books as well.

The Edges are grouped by type to help during character creation. Unless an Edge specifically says otherwise, it may only be selected once.

Rank: Below each Edge is the Rank that you must have to purchase it. A Novice character can't buy a Legendary Edge, for instance. A character may always purchase an Edge of a Rank lower than his.

Improved Edges: Some Edges also have improved effects if you purchase additional "levels" in them, such as Attractive and Very Attractive, or Rich and Filthy Rich. To buy an Improved Edge, you must have all previous versions of an Edge. You must choose Rich before buying Filthy Rich, for example.

BACKGROUND EDGES

These Edges are hereditary and background advantages that may usually be purchased only during character creation.

If a player has a particularly good reason for picking up a Background Edge during play, he should talk it over with the GM. If she agrees that it makes sense, the character may choose the Edge when leveling just like any other. A character might choose the Attractive Edge, for example, by cleaning herself up, getting a makeover, and generally paying more attention to her looks. Characters might be able to gain the Arcane Background Edge as well, should they find a book of forbidden knowledge or train under another arcane type in their party.

ALERTNESS

Requirements: Novice

Not much gets by your hero. He's very observant and perceptive, and adds +2 to his Notice rolls to hear, see, or otherwise sense the world around him.

AMBIDEXTROUS

Requirements: Novice, Agility d8+

Your hero is as deft with his left hand as he is with his right. He may ignore the –2 penalty for using his off-hand.

ARCANE BACKGROUND

Requirements: Novice, Special

This is the Edge your character must purchase to have any sort of magical, psionic, or other supernatural ability.

See Chapter Four for a complete description.

ARCANE RESISTANCE

Requirements: Novice, Spirit d8+

Your character is particularly resistant to magic (or psionics, or weird science, etc), whether by nature or by heritage. He acts as if he had 2 points of Armor when hit by damage-causing arcane powers, and adds +2 to his Trait rolls when resisting opposed powers. Even friendly arcane powers must subtract this modifier to affect the resistant hero.

IMPROVED ARCANE RESISTANCE

Requirements: Novice, Arcane Resistance

As above but Armor and resistance are increased to 4.

ATTRACTIVE

Requirements: Novice, Vigor d6+

Your hero or heroine is very handsome or beautiful. His or her Charisma is increased by +2.

VERY ATTRACTIVE

Requirements: Novice, Attractive

Your hero or heroine is drop-dead gorgeous. His or her Charisma is increased by +4 total.

BERSERK

Requirements: Novice

Immediately after suffering a wound (including a Shaken result from physical damage), your hero must make a Smarts roll or go berserk.

While Berserk, his Parry is reduced by 2 but he adds +2 to all Fighting and Strength rolls (including melee damage) and his Toughness. The warrior ignores all wound modifiers while berserk, but cannot use any skills, Edges, or maneuvers that require concentration, including Shooting and Taunt, but not Intimidation.

Berserkers attack with reckless abandon. Anytime his Fighting die is a 1 (regardless of his Wild Die), he hits a random adjacent target, (not the original target). The attack may hit friend as well as foe. If there are no other adjacent targets, the blow simply misses.

The Berserker may end his rage by doing nothing (not even moving) for one full action and making a Smarts roll at –2.

BRAWNY

Requirements: Novice, Strength and Vigor d6+

Your hero is very large or perhaps just very fit. Either way, his bulk resists damage better than most. Add +1 to your Toughness.

In addition, your hero can carry more than most proportional to his Strength. He can carry 8 times his Strength in pounds without penalty instead of the usual 5 times his Strength.

FAST HEALER

Requirements: Novice, Vigor d8+

Your hero heals quickly. He may add +2 to his Vigor rolls when checking for natural healing.

LUCK

Requirements: Novice

The player seems to be blessed by fate. He draws 1 extra benny at the beginning of each game session, allowing him to succeed at important tasks more often than most, and survive incredible dangers.

GREAT LUCK

Requirements: Novice, Luck

The player draws 2 extra bennies instead of 1 for his luck at the start of each session.

NOBLE

Requirements: Novice

Those born of noble blood have many perks in life, but often have just as many responsibilities. Nobles have high status in their societies, are entitled to special treatment from their foes, gain +2 Charisma, and also have the Rich Edge. This gives the hero several Edges for the price of one, but the responsibilities more than offset the additional perks. Nobles often have troops under their control, as well as land, a family home, and other assets. All of this must be determined by the GM, and balanced by the grave responsibilities the character faces. As an example, a character in a fantasy campaign might have a company of swordsmen, a small keep, and even a magical sword he inherited from his father. But he also has an entire county to manage, criminals to judge, justice to mete out, and a jealous neighbor who covets his lands and constantly plots against him at court.

QUICK

Requirements: Novice, Agility d8+

Your character was born with lightning-fast reflexes and a cool head. Whenever you are dealt a 5 or lower in combat, you may discard and draw again until you get a card higher than 5.

Level Headed characters draw their additional card and take the best *before* using their Quick Edge.

RICH

Requirements: Novice

Whether your hero was born with a silver spoon in his mouth or earned it through hard work, he's got more money than most others.

The guidelines below are listed in modern terms so that your GM can figure out exactly what it means in campaign worlds of his own creation.

Rich heroes start with three times the normal starting funds for the setting. If a regular income is appropriate for this setting, the hero receives the modern day equivalent of a $75,000 annual salary.

FILTHY RICH

Requirements: Novice, Rich or Noble

This character is very wealthy. He has five times the starting funds for the setting and, if appropriate, a yearly income of around $250,000.

Wealthier characters should have a very complete background as well. This needs to be worked out with the GM, and comes with many more assets as well as onerous responsibilities.

Combat Edges

These Edges are designed to help your hero do one simple thing—kick butt!

Block

Requirements: Seasoned, Fighting d8+

Heroes who engage in frequent hand-to-hand combat are far more skilled in personal defense than most others. They've learned not only how to attack, but how to block their opponent's blows as well. A hero with this Edge adds +1 to his Parry.

Improved Block

Requirements: Veteran, Block

As above, but the hero adds +2 to his Parry.

Combat Reflexes

Requirements: Seasoned

Your hero recovers quickly from shock and trauma. He adds +2 to his Spirit roll when attempting to recover from being Shaken.

Dodge

Requirements: Seasoned, Agility d8+

Some heroes are crafty types who know how to get out of harm's way. This Edge allows them to use cover, movement, and concealment to make them harder to hit. Unless they are the victim of a surprise attack and taken completely unaware, attackers must subtract 1 from their Shooting or Throwing rolls when targeting them.

Characters who attempt to evade area effect attacks may add +1 to their Agility roll as well (when allowed).

Improved Dodge

Requirements: Veteran, Dodge

As above but attackers subtract 2 from their attack rolls, and the character adds +2 to evade area effect weapons when allowed.

First Strike

Requirements: Novice, Agility d8+

Once per turn the hero gets a free Fighting attack against a single foe who moves adjacent to him. This automatically interrupts the opponent's action, and does not cost the hero his action if he is on Hold or has not yet acted this round.

Improved First Strike

Requirements: Heroic, First Strike

As above but the hero may make one free attack against each and every foe who moves adjacent to him.

Fleet-Footed

Requirements: Novice, Agility d6+

The hero's Pace is increased by +2 and he rolls a d10 instead of a d6 when running.

Florentine

Requirements: Novice, Agility d8+, Fighting d8+

A character trained to fight "Florentine" is a master at wielding two weapons at once. He adds +1 to his Fighting rolls versus an opponent with a single weapon and no shield. In addition, opponents subtract 1 from any "gang up" bonuses they would normally get against the hero as his two flashing blades parry their blows.

Frenzy

Requirements: Seasoned; Fighting d10+

Frenzied fighters make fast and furious melee attacks, sacrificing finesse for raw speed. This allows them to make an extra Fighting attack per round at a –2 penalty to all Fighting rolls. This attack must be taken at the same time as another Fighting attack though it may target any two foes adjacent to the hero (Wild Cards roll two Fighting dice and one Wild Die). The –2 penalty is subtracted from all attacks.

A character armed with two weapons still only makes one extra attack.

IMPROVED FRENZY

Requirements: Veteran, Frenzy

As above but the character may ignore the –2 Frenzy penalty.

GIANT KILLER

Requirements: Veteran

The bigger they are, the harder they are to kill. At least for most. But your hero knows how to find the weak points in massive creatures.

Your hero does +1d6 damage when attacking creatures three sizes or more larger than himself. An ogre (Size+3) with this ability, for example, gains the bonus only against creatures of Size +6 or greater. A human Giant Killer (Size 0), can claim the bonus against the ogre, however.

HARD TO KILL

Requirements: Wild Card, Novice, Spirit d8+

Your hero has more lives than a truckload of cats. When forced to make Vigor rolls due to Incapacitation, he may ignore his wound modifiers. This only applies to Vigor rolls called for by these tables—he still suffers from wound modifiers for other Trait rolls normally.

HARDER TO KILL

Requirements: Veteran, Hard to Kill

Your hero is tougher to kill than Rasputin.

If he is ever "killed," roll a die. On an odd result, he's dead as usual. On an even roll, he's Incapacitated but somehow escapes death. He may be captured, stripped of all his belongings, or mistakenly left for dead, but he somehow survives.

LEVEL HEADED

Requirements: Seasoned, Smarts d8+

Fighters who can keep their cool when everyone else is running for cover are deadly customers in combat.

A hero with this Edge draws an additional action card in combat and acts on the best of the draw.

IMPROVED LEVEL HEADED

Requirements: Seasoned, Level Headed

As above but the hero draws 3 cards.

MARKSMAN

Requirements: Seasoned

The hero excels at taking controlled, measured shots. If he does not move in a turn, he may fire as if he took the aim maneuver. Marksman may never be used with a rate of fire greater than 1.

Marksman works with both Shooting and Throwing.

NERVES OF STEEL

Requirements: Wild Card, Novice, Vigor d8+

Your hero has learned to fight on through the most intense pain. He may ignore 1 point of wound penalties.

Improved Nerves of Steel

Requirements: Novice, Nerves of Steel

The hero ignores 2 points of wound penalties.

No Mercy

Requirements: Seasoned

The character may spend a benny to reroll any one damage roll. Against area-effect attacks, each benny spent applies to one target.

Quick Draw

Requirements: Novice, Agility d8+

This Edge allows a hero to draw a weapon and ignore the usual −2 to his attack that round. If the character must make an Agility roll to draw a weapon (see the combat section for more details), he adds +2 to the roll.

Rock and Roll!

Requirements: Seasoned, Shooting d8+

Some veteran shooters have learned how to compensate for the recoil of fully-automatic weapons. If a character with this Edge does not move, he may ignore the recoil penalty for firing a weapon on fully automatic.

Steady Hands

Requirements: Novice, Agility d8+

Your hero ignores the "unstable platform" penalty for firing from the backs of animals or while riding in moving vehicles.

Sweep

Requirements: Novice, Strength d8+, Fighting d8+

Sweep allows a character to make a single Fighting attack and apply it against all adjacent targets at a −2 penalty. Resolve each damage roll separately. Allies are affected by such attacks as well, so heroes must be careful when and how they use this powerful ability. A character may not use Sweep in the same round she uses Frenzy.

Improved Sweep

Requirements: Veteran, Sweep

As above but the hero may ignore the −2 penalty.

Trademark Weapon

Requirements: Novice, Fighting or Shooting of d10+

The hero knows one unique weapon (*Excalibur, Old Betsy, Sting*) like the back of his hand. When using that weapon, he adds +1 to his Fighting, Shooting, or Throwing rolls. A hero can take this Edge multiple times, applying it to a different weapon each time. If a Trademark Weapon is lost, the hero can replace it, but the benefit of the Edge doesn't kick in for two game weeks.

Improved Trademark Weapon

Requirements: Veteran, Trademark Weapon

As above but the bonus when using the weapon increases to +2.

COMMAND

Requirements: Novice, Smarts d6+

Command is the ability to give clear instructions to surrounding allies and enforce your hero's will upon them. This makes your character's compatriots more willing to fight on despite their wounds, and so adds +1 to their Spirit rolls to recover from being Shaken.

FERVOR

Requirements: Veteran, Spirit d8+, Command

A simple phrase uttered by a great leader can sometimes have momentous results. A leader with this ability can inspire his men to bloody fervor by yelling a motto, slogan, or other inspirational words.

Those in the command radius add +1 to their Fighting damage rolls.

HOLD THE LINE!

Requirements: Seasoned, Smarts d8+, Command

This Edge strengthens the will of the men under the hero's command. The troops add +1 to their Toughness.

INSPIRE

Requirements: Seasoned, Command

Leaders with exceptional reputations and experience in battle inspire the soldiers around them. They add +2 to the Spirit rolls when recovering from being Shaken (this already includes the original +1 bonus for the Command Edge). This greatly improves the chances of men recovering from light wounds or poor morale that might normally take them out of the action.

NATURAL LEADER

Requirements: Novice, Spirit d8+, Command

This Edge signifies a special link between a leader and his men. With it, he may share his bennies with any troops under his command.

TWO-FISTED

Requirements: Novice, Agility d8+

A Two-Fisted hero isn't ambidextrous—he's simply learned to fight with two weapons (or both fists) at once. When attacking with a weapon in each hand, he rolls each attack separately but ignores the multi-action penalty.

LEADERSHIP EDGES

Leadership Edges allow characters to make better use of NPC allies in battle, making them more effective, reliable, or durable.

These Edges apply only to subordinate Extras within 5" (the "command radius"). Wild Card characters are rarely affected by Leadership Edges—they're far too independent-minded to be driven by others, except for the strongest leaders).

Leadership Edges are not cumulative from multiple commanders. Troops cannot benefit from two leaders with the Command Edge, for example. They could benefit from two different Edges, however, such as Command and Fervor, even if possessed by two different leaders.

Power Edges

Power Edges are for those with Arcane Backgrounds. See the Powers section for more information on each type of Arcane Background, how to use them, and the powers available.

New Power

Requirements: Novice, Arcane Background

An arcane character may learn a new power by choosing this Edge (which may be taken multiple times). He may choose from any powers normally available to his particular Arcane Background.

Power Points

Requirements: Novice, Arcane Background

Wizards, weird scientists, and other arcane types always want more power. This Edge grants them an additional 5 Power Points.

Power Points may be selected more than once, but only once per Rank.

Rapid Recharge

Requirements: Seasoned, Spirit d6+, Arcane Background

This Edge allows an arcane character to regain 1 Power Point every 30 minutes.

Improved Rapid Recharge

Requirements: Veteran, Rapid Recharge

The character regains 1 Power Point every 15 minutes.

Soul Drain

Rank: Seasoned, Arcane Background (any but Weird Science), Knowledge (arcana) d10+

Spellcasters, mentalists, and other arcane types in dire need of Power Points may use this Edge to drain energy from their own souls.

To use this dangerous ability, the arcane character first decides how many Power Points he wants to draw from himself. Then he makes a Spirit roll minus the number of points he's trying to drain. (This is a free action.) On a Spirit total of 1 or less, the character suffers a wound and falls unconscious for 1d6 hours. On a failure, the character suffers a wound. On a success or better, the character gets the points he needed and may attempt to cast a spell with them immediately (they may not be saved).

PROFESSIONAL EDGES

Professional Edges are very special abilities that reflect many years of practicing a particular trade. In some cases they may also represent special blessings from higher powers as well.

These Edges help you create a character who is far more competent in his chosen field than most others—far more than just having a d12 in that occupation's skills. If you want to make a typical Mad Scientist, for example, you could create a character normally, then give him the Gadgeteer and Mr. Fix It Edges. Similarly, a priest from a typical swords and sorcery game has Arcane Background (Miracles) as well as the Champion and Holy Warrior Edges.

Professional Edges represent many years of training so their Requirements are quite high. Players may purchase Professional Edges after character creation, but should usually lead up to it story-wise by practicing the affected trade during down-time or in between adventures. The time spent acquiring one of these abilities is subjective and up to the Game Master, but makes the game much more believable if a little narrative time is spent training.

Stacking: Bonuses to the same Trait from different Professional Edges do not stack. If you make a hero with both the Woodsman and the Thief Edges, for example, he gains +2 to his Stealth skill—not +4.

ACE

Requirements: Novice, Agility d8+

Aces are special pilots and drivers who feel more comfortable behind the wheel, throttle, or flightstick than on their own two feet.

Aces add +2 to Boating, Driving, and Piloting rolls. In addition, they may also spend bennies to make soak rolls for any vehicle or vessel they control. This is a Boating, Driving, or Piloting roll at −2 (cancelling their usual +2). Each success and raise negates a wound and any critical hit that would have resulted from it.

ACROBAT

Requirements: Novice, Agility d8+, Strength d6+

Those who have formal training in the acrobatic arts or are naturally agile may take this Edge. It adds +2 to all Agility rolls made to perform acrobatic maneuvers (including Trick maneuvers), and also adds +1 to a character's Parry as long as he has no encumbrance penalty.

Example: Buck wants to leap over an angry crocodile and attempt to interrupt the enemy shaman who's about to cast some dark spell. If Buck had the Acrobat Edge, he'd add +2 to his Agility roll to leap over the croc, but not to the opposed Agility test to try and interrupt the shaman's action.

CHAMPION

Requirements: Novice, Arcane Background (Miracles), Spirit d8+, Strength d6+, Vigor d8+, Faith d6+, Fighting d8+

Champions are holy (or unholy) men and women chosen to fight for a particular deity or religion. Most are pious souls ready and willing to lay down their lives for a greater cause, but some may have been born into the profession and follow their path with some reluctance.

Champions fight the forces of darkness (or good). They add +2 damage when attacking supernaturally evil (or good) creatures, and have +2 Toughness when suffering damage from supernaturally evil (or good) sources, including arcane powers and the weapons, claws, or teeth of such creatures.

GADGETEER

Requirements: Novice, Arcane Background (Weird Science), Smarts d8+, Repair d8+, Weird Science d8+, at least two other scientific Knowledge skills at d6+

These mechanical gurus are so technically savvy they can quickly build a machine to handle nearly any situation.

Once per game session, a gadgeteer can create a "jury-rigged" device from spare parts. The device functions just like any other Weird Science device, and uses any power available to Weird Scientists in that setting (though this is still subject to Rank restrictions). It has half the inventor's Power Points, and once these are used up, the gadget burns out and does not recharge. The inventor must have access to some parts and a reasonable amount of time (GM's call, but at least 1d20 minutes) to create the gizmo.

HOLY/UNHOLY WARRIOR

Requirements: Novice, Arcane Background (Miracles), Spirit d8+, Faith d6+

Acolytes, clerics, paladins, holy slayers, and other avatars of the gods are frequently tasked with battling the forces of evil in the mortal world. This Edge gives them a slight advantage against such foes.

As an action, a priest or other holy person may call upon his chosen deity to repulse supernaturally evil creatures, such as the undead, demons, and the like. It also works on evil characters with the Arcane Background (Miracles) Edge.

Repulsing evil costs 1 Power Point and has a range of the character's Spirit. Targeted creatures within that range must make a Spirit roll. Failure means the creature is Shaken; a 1 means it is destroyed. Wild Cards suffer an automatic Wound instead.

A character may also be an Unholy Warrior working for the forces of evil. In this case, he repulses good creatures, such as angels, paladins, or good characters with Arcane Background (Miracles).

INVESTIGATOR

Requirements: Novice, Smarts d8+, Investigation d8+, Streetwise d8+

Investigators are characters who have spent a great deal of time researching ancient legends, working the streets, or deducing devilish mysteries. Some of these heroes are actual Private Investigators for hire while others may be sleuthing mages in a fantasy world or perhaps inquisitive college professors stumbling upon Things

In addition, given a few simple tools, props, or devices, he can generally rig devices to help escape from death-traps, weapons to match some bizarre need, or otherwise create something that's needed when such a thing isn't actually present. The extent of this is completely up to the Game Master, but creativity should be rewarded, particularly in dire situations where few other answers are possible.

MENTALIST

Requirements: Novice, Arcane Background (Psionics), Smarts d8+, Psionics d6+

Mentalists are masters of mind control and psionics. Some are pulp heroes, others are trained in secret government academies to root out traitors. Their frequent toying with human minds gives them a +2 on any opposed Psionics roll, whether they are using their powers against a foe or are trying to defend against a rival mentalist.

MR. FIX IT

Requirements: Novice, Arcane Background (Weird Science), Smarts d10+, Repair d8+, Weird Science d8+, at least two other scientific Knowledge skills at d6+

The inventor adds +2 to his Repair rolls. With a raise, he halves the time normally required to fix something. This means that if a particular Repair job already states that a raise repairs it in half the time, a Mr. Fix It could finish the job in one-quarter the time with a raise.

SCHOLAR

Requirements: Novice, d8+ in affected skill

Learned professors, devoted students, and amateur enthusiasts spend months of their lives studying particular fields. They become experts in these fields, and rarely fail to answer questions in their particular area of expertise.

Man was not Meant to Know in the dark of night. Investigators add +2 to Investigation and Streetwise rolls, as well as Notice rolls made to search through evidence.

JACK-OF-ALL-TRADES

Requirements: Novice, Smarts d10+

Through advanced schooling, book-learning, computer-enhanced skill programs, or just amazing intuitive perception, your hero has a talent for picking up skills on the fly. There is little he can't figure out given a little time and a dash of luck.

Any time he makes an unskilled roll for a Smarts-based skill, he may do so at d4 instead of the usual d4–2.

MCGYVER

Requirements: Novice, Smarts d6+, Repair d6+, Notice d8+

This character can improvise something when the need for a tool arises. He suffers no negative penalties on Trait rolls for lack of equipment in most situations.

Pick any two Knowledge skills that you have a d8 or better in. Add +2 to your total whenever these skills are used. Yes, those who study military history have a natural edge when commanding troops in mass battles—a +2 to a Knowledge (Battle) roll can mean the difference between a rousing victory and a crushing defeat.

THIEF

Requirements: Novice, Agility d8+, Climb d6+, Lockpick d6+, Stealth d8+

Thieves specialize in deceit, treachery, and acrobatics. They can be invaluable where traps must be detected, walls must be climbed, and locks must be picked.

Thieves add +2 to Climb, Lockpick, and Stealth rolls. The bonus to Stealth does not apply when the character is in a wilderness environment—only in urban areas.

WIZARD

Requirements: Novice, Arcane Background (Magic), Smarts d8+, Knowledge (arcana) d8+, Spellcasting d6+

Wizards range from young apprentices to frighteningly powerful supreme sorcerers. They are often physically weak, however, and do not have the divine powers or healing abilities of priestly spellcasters. What they lack in spiritual favor, however, they more than make up for in utility and eldritch might. Wizards can cast the widest variety of spells, and if advanced wisely, have a wide variety of Power Edges to further increase their awesome abilities.

Wizards learn their craft in formalized institutions or under the tutelage of experienced masters. Each raise a wizard gets on his Spellcasting roll reduces the cost of the spell by 1 Power Point. The wizard must have the points available to cast the spell in the first place before rolling.

WOODSMAN

Requirements: Novice, Spirit d6+, Survival d8+, Tracking d8+

Woodsmen are rangers, scouts, and hunters who are more at home in the wilderness than in urban areas. They are skilled trackers and scouts, and know how to live off the land for months at a time.

Woodsmen gain +2 to Tracking, Survival, and Stealth rolls made in the wilderness (not towns, ruins, or underground).

SOCIAL EDGES

Getting people to do what you want is a critical skill in most any setting. These Edges help your hero do just that.

CHARISMATIC

Requirements: Novice, Spirit d8+

Your hero has learned how to work with others, even those who might be somewhat opposed to him or his efforts. This adds +2 to his Charisma.

COMMON BOND

Requirements: Wild Card, Novice, Spirit d8+

This Edge signifies a special link between close companions—such as a typical party. It doesn't matter whether or not the characters get along perfectly or not, they've just formed a close and common bond during their epic adventures.

A character with this Edge may freely give his bennies to any other Wild Card he can communicate with. This represents the character giving his verbal or spiritual support to the ally. The player should say what his character is doing to give the support. The gesture could be as complex as a rousing speech, or as simple as a knowing nod.

CONNECTIONS

Requirements: Novice

Whether it's to the Feds, the cops, the Mob, or some big corporation, your heroine knows someone on the inside – someone who is willing to lend her a hand on occasion (usually once per game session).

This Edge may be taken more than once, but each time must be applied to a different organization. The GM should also ensure the organization is limited to a single, unique organization. A hero may, for instance, have Connections (US Army), but he shouldn't have a blanket Connection (Military).

To use a character's Connection requires that she first get in touch with one of her contacts. This requires a Streetwise roll. Failure means the particular contact wasn't available, their cell phone wasn't on, or they were otherwise tied up.

Once in contact, the hero must make a Persuasion roll. The GM should feel free to modify both the Persuasion roll and any results based on the circumstances.

A failure indicates the heroine's contacts just couldn't come through this time, or perhaps just weren't persuaded that their help was really necessary.

On a success, the contact might share information, but won't do anything too risky to help.

On a raise, the contact is willing to leak sensitive information, but stops short of outright betrayal.

Two or more raises means the heroine has pushed the right buttons and can count on serious help. The Connection will risk serious consequences for the heroine. If she needs financial assistance, the contact may provide a little more than he's comfortable with. If the heroine asks for muscle, the contact delivers either one expert (a safe-cracker, wheel-man, security expert, etc) or five average fighter-types for the contact's particular organization (a mob boss sends five thugs, the Army sends five infantrymen, etc.).

STRONG WILLED

Requirements: Novice, Intimidate d6+, Taunt d6+

Characters with strong willpower use their voice, steely stares, or quick wits to unnerve their opponents.

Strong Willed adds +2 to a character's Intimidate and Taunt rolls, as well as his Spirit and Smarts rolls when resisting Tests of Will attacks.

Weird Edges

Weird Edges are slightly supernatural, and are only appropriate in games with those elements. The Game Master must decide if characters can gain access to these benefits. A few common Edges are listed below. Individual settings offer more Weird Edges specifically tailored for that world.

Beast Bond

Requirements: Novice

Some heroes can exert incredible will over their animal companion. These characters may spend their own bennies for any animals under their control, including mounts, pet dogs, familiars, and so on.

Beast Master

Requirements: Novice, Spirit d8+

Animals like your hero, and won't attack him unless he attacks them first or they are enraged for some reason. His "animal magnetism" is so great he's attracted a loyal animal of some sort as well. This is typically a dog, wolf, or raptor of some sort, though the GM may allow other companions if it fits the setting. If the beast is killed, another comes in 2d6 days if possible.

Danger Sense

Requirements: Novice

Your hero can sense when something bad is about to happen. Anytime he's about to be the victim of a surprise attack, ambush, or other nasty surprise, he gets a Notice roll at −2 just before the attack or event occurs. If successful, the character knows something is about to happen and may take appropriate action against it. This means the hero is on Hold for the first round of a combat.

Should the hero fail his roll, he still follows the normal Surprise rules, if applicable.

Healer

Requirements: Novice, Spirit d8+

A character with this Edge adds +2 to all Healing rolls, whether natural or magical in nature. Up to five companions traveling with a Healer add the bonus to their natural healing rolls as well.

Wild Card Edges

The following Edges work only when the character is dealt a Joker during combat. The Edge's effects are in addition to the usual effects of being dealt a Joker.

Dead Shot

Requirements: Wild Card, Seasoned, Shooting/Throwing d10+

The character doubles his total damage when making a successful Shooting or Throwing attack this round.

Mighty Blow

Requirements: Wild Card, Seasoned, Fighting d10+

The character doubles his total damage when making a successful Fighting attack this round.

Power Surge

Requirements: Wild Card, Seasoned, arcane skill d10+

This Edge is for those characters with Arcane Backgrounds. When dealt a Joker, the character recovers 2d6 Power Points. He may not exceed his usual limit.

Legendary Edges

The Edges listed below are out of the regular order because few campaigns get to this level. Most Legendary Edges are very specific to their campaign world—such as gaining a stronghold or divine favor—but a few fit most anywhere, as shown below.

Followers

Requirements: Wild Card, Legendary

Heroes often acquire dedicated warbands, "merry men," or others who voluntarily follow the hero on his adventures.

Each time this Edge is chosen, 5 followers join the hero's band. Casualties are not automatically replaced, so a hero may need to choose this Edge again on occasion to replenish his losses.

The followers must have some way to eat and earn income, and generally want a piece of whatever loot, treasure, or other rewards the hero acquires. Otherwise, they are completely dedicated to their idol and risk their lives for him under any normal conditions. In general, they won't knowingly throw their lives away, but special circumstances or those who have been with the hero for a few years might.

The GM determines the followers' statistics, but in general, use the Soldier archetype presented later in this book. Followers generally come with only basic equipment depending on their particular setting (warriors in fantasy come with at least leather armor and short swords, for example). The hero must purchase any additional equipment for his Followers himself.

PROFESSIONAL

Requirements: Legendary, d12 in affected Trait.

The character is an expert at a particular Trait. His Trait becomes d12+1. This Edge may be selected more than once, but it may never be applied to the same Trait twice.

EXPERT

Requirements: Legendary, Professional in affected Trait

As above, but the Trait increases to d12+2.

MASTER

Requirements: Wild Card, Legendary, Expert in affected Trait.

The character's Wild Die increases to a d10 when rolling a particular Trait of his choice. This Edge may be chosen multiple times, though it only affects a particular Trait once.

SIDEKICK

Requirements: Wild Card, Legendary

A character who triumphs over evil time and time again becomes an inspiration to others. Eventually, one of these young crusaders may attempt to join the hero in his epic quests.

The hero gains a Novice Rank sidekick. The sidekick is a Wild Card, gains experience as usual, and has abilities that complement or mimic his hero's.

In general, the player character should control his sidekick just like any other allied character. Of course, the sidekick may occasionally cause trouble (by getting captured, running into danger when he's not supposed to, etc.). The player should be prepared for his "Edge" to occasionally become a "Hindrance."

If the sidekick dies, he isn't replaced unless the hero chooses this Edge again.

TOUGH AS NAILS

Requirements: Legendary

Your hero is a grizzled veteran. Increase his Toughness by +1.

IMPROVED TOUGH AS NAILS

Requirements: Legendary, Tough as Nails

Increase your hero's Toughness by another +1.

WEAPON MASTER

Requirements: Legendary, Fighting d12

Increase your hero's Parry by +1.

MASTER OF ARMS

Requirements: Legendary, Weapon Master

Increase your hero's Parry by another +1.

ADVANCEMENT

At the end of each game session (usually 4-6 hours of gaming), the GM awards 1 to 3 Experience Points to everyone in the group, based on these guidelines.

EXPERIENCE AWARDS

Award	Situation
1	The group accomplished very little or had a very short session.
2	The group had more successes than failures.
3	The group succeeded greatly, and their adventure had a significant impact on the overall story.

RANKS

As a character gains more Experience Points, he goes up in "Rank." This is a rough measure of how powerful the hero is. As characters progress in experience, new Ranks allow access to more powerful Edges.

RANK TABLE

Experience Points	Rank
0-19	Novice
20-39	Seasoned
40-59	Veteran
60-79	Heroic
80+	Legendary

Every 5 points accumulated grants a hero an Advance. An Advance lets a character levels do one of the following:

• Gain a new Edge.
• Increase a skill that is equal to or greater than its linked attribute by one die type.
• Increase two skills that are lower than their linked attributes by one die type each.
• Buy a new skill at d4.
• Increase one attribute by a die type.*

*You may only choose this option once per rank. No Trait may be raised above a d12 (but see the Professional and Expert Legendary Edges). Legendary characters may raise an attribute every other Advance.

STARTING WITH EXPERIENCED CHARACTERS

If the GM lets you make a character who has already earned some experience, simply make a character as usual and then grant her that many Advances. A Veteran character, for example, has 40 Experience Points, so you would make a normal character and grant her eight Advances.

Additional goods, equipment, or other assets must be determined by the Game Master and the particular setting. As a quick rule of thumb, a character's starting funds double with each Rank after Novice.

Replacement Characters: When a character dies, his new hero begins play with half the Experience Points his former hero had (round down). If a character died with 17 Experience Points, for example, his replacement enters play with 8 points.

LEGENDARY CHARACTERS

Legendary characters are major forces in their worlds, and often have political power and influence as well as a host of Edges to defeat those who oppose them.

Once a hero reaches Legendary status, the rules for Advances change a bit. The character now Advances every time he accumulates 10 Experience Points instead of 5, but a world of new Edges opens up to him as well. "Legendary Edges" allow heroes to accumulate followers, build castles, start massive corporations, and otherwise become major players in their campaign world.

Legendary characters may also choose to improve an attribute every other Advance. A few Legendary Edges are included in this book. Many more are quite specific to their particular campaign worlds, and so are covered in upcoming Savage Settings.

Summaries

Character Creation Summary

1) Race
• Choose any race available in your setting.

2) Traits
• Your hero starts with a d4 in each attribute, and has 5 points with which to raise them. Raising an attribute a die type costs 1 point.

• You have 15 points for skills.

• Each die type in a skill costs 1 point up to the linked attribute. Going over the linked attribute costs 2 points per level.

• Charisma is equal to the total bonuses or penalties given by Edges and Hindrances.

• Pace is 6".

• Parry is equal to 2 plus half Fighting.

• Toughness is equal to 2 plus half Vigor. Go ahead and add the bonus granted by the armor worn on your torso to this value as well for speed's sake, but remember it may not count if attacks target other parts of the body.

3) Edges & Hindrances
• You gain additional points for taking up to one Major Hindrance and two Minor Hindrances.

For 2 points you can:
• Gain another attribute point.
• Choose an Edge.

For 1 point you can:
• Gain another skill point.
• Increase starting funds by 100%

4) Gear
• Start with $500 unless your setting book says otherwise.

5) Background Details
• Fill in any other background details you care to add.

Skills

Skill	Attribute
Boating	Agility
Climbing	Strength
Driving	Agility
Fighting	Agility
Gambling	Smarts
Guts	Spirit
Healing	Smarts
Intimidation	Spirit
Investigation	Smarts
Knowledge	Smarts
Lockpicking	Agility
Notice	Smarts
Persuasion	Spirit
Piloting	Agility
Repair	Smarts
Riding	Agility
Shooting	Agility
Stealth	Agility
Streetwise	Smarts
Survival	Smarts
Swimming	Agility
Taunt	Smarts
Throwing	Agility
Tracking	Smarts

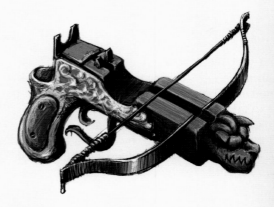

Hindrances Summary

Hindrance	Type	Effects
All Thumbs	Minor	−2 Repair; Roll of 1 causes malfunction
Anemic	Minor	−2 Vigor to resist sickness, disease, poison, environment
Arrogant	Major	Must humiliate opponent, challenge the 'leader'
Bad Eyes	Minor/Major	−2 to attack or notice something more than 5" distant
Bad Luck	Major	One less benny per session
Big Mouth	Minor	Unable to keep a secret, blabs at the worst time
Blind	Major	−6 to all actions that rely on vision; −2 on social rolls, gain additional Edge
Bloodthirsty	Major	Never takes prisoners
Cautious	Minor	Character is overly careful
Clueless	Major	−2 to most Common Knowledge rolls
Code of Honor	Major	Character keeps his word and acts like a gentleman
Curious	Major	Character wants to know about everything
Death Wish	Minor	Hero wants to die after completing some task
Delusional	Minor/Major	Character suffers from grave delusions
Doubting Thomas	Minor	Character doesn't believe in the supernatural
Elderly	Major	Pace −1, −1 to Strength and Vigor die types; 5 extra skill points for any skill linked to Smarts
Enemy	Minor/Major	Character has a recurring nemesis of some sort
Greedy	Minor/Major	Character is obsessed with wealth
Habit	Minor/Major	Charisma −1; Fatigue rolls when deprived of Major Habits
Hard of Hearing	Minor/Major	−2 to Notice sounds; automatic failure if completely deaf
Heroic	Major	Character always helps those in need
Illiterate	Minor	Hero is unable to read or write
Lame	Major	−2 Pace and running die is a d4
Loyal	Minor	The hero tries to never betray or disappoint his friends
Mean	Minor	−2 to his Charisma for ill-temper and surliness
Obese	Minor	+1 Toughness, −1 Pace, d4 running die
One Arm	Major	−4 to tasks requiring two arms
One Eye	Major	−1 Charisma, −2 to rolls requiring depth perception
One Leg	Major	Pace −2, d4 running die, −2 to rolls requiring mobility, −2 to Swimming skill
Outsider	Minor	−2 Charisma, treated badly by those of dominant society
Overconfident	Major	The hero believes he can do anything
Pacifist	Minor/Major	Character fights only in self-defense as a Minor Hindrance; won't harm living creatures as Major Hindrance
Phobia	Minor/Major	−2 or −4 to Trait tests when near the phobia
Poverty	Minor	Half starting funds, inability to hang onto future income
Quirk	Minor	Character has some minor but persistent foible
Small	Major	−1 Toughness
Stubborn	Minor	Hero always wants his way
Ugly	Minor	−2 Charisma due to appearance
Vengeful	Minor/Major	Character holds a grudge; will kill as a Major Hindrance
Vow	Minor/Major	A pledge to a group, deity, or religion
Wanted	Minor/Major	The character is a criminal of some sort
Yellow	Major	The character is cowardly and suffers −2 to his Guts rolls
Young	Major	3 points for Attributes, 10 skill points, +1 benny per session

EDGES SUMMARY

Edge	Requirements	Effects
Ace	N, A d8	+2 to Boating, Driving, Piloting; may make soak rolls for vehicle at −2
Acrobat	N, A d8, St d6	+2 to nimbleness-based Agility rolls; +1 Parry if unencumbered
Alertness*	N	+2 Notice
Ambidextrous*	N, A d8	Ignore −2 penalty for using off-hand
Arcane Background*	N, Special	Allows access to supernatural powers
Arcane Resistance*	N, Sp d8	Armor 2 vs. magic, +2 to resist powers
Imp. Arcane Res	N, Arcane Res.	Armor 4 vs. magic, +4 to resist magic effects
Attractive*	N, V d6	Charisma +2
Very Attractive*	N, Attractive	Charisma +4
Beast Bond	N	Character may spend bennies for his animals
Beast Master	N, Sp d8	You gain an animal companion
Berserk*	N	See text
Block	S, Fighting d8	Parry +1
Improved Block	V, Block	Parry +2
Brawny*	N, St d6, V d6	Toughness +1; load limit is 8 x Str
Champion	N, See text	+2 damage / Toughness vs. supernatural evil
Charismatic	N, Sp d8	Charisma +2
Combat Reflexes	S	+2 to recover from being Shaken
Command	N, Sm d6	+1 to troops recovering from being Shaken
Common Bond	WC, N, Sp d8	May give bennies to companions
Connections	N	Call upon powerful friends
Danger Sense	N	Notice at −2 to detect surprise attacks/danger
Dead Shot	WC, S, Shoot/Throw d10	Double ranged damage when dealt Joker
Dodge	S, A d8	−1 to be hit with ranged attacks
Improved Dodge	V, Dodge	−2 to be hit with ranged attacks
Fast Healer*	N, V d8	+2 to natural healing rolls
Fervor	V, Sp d8, Command	+1 melee damage to troops in command
First Strike	N, A d8	May attack one foe who moves adjacent
Imp. First Strike	H, First Strike	May attack every foe who moves adjacent
Fleet-Footed	N, A d6	+2 Pace, d10 running die instead of d6
Florentine	N, A d8, Fighting d8	+1 vs. foes with single weapon and no shield; ignore 1 point of gang up bonus
Followers	L, WC	Attract 5 henchmen
Frenzy	S, Fighting d10	1 extra Fighting attack at −2
Imp. Frenzy	V, Frenzy	As above but no penalty
Gadgeteer	N, See text	May "jury-rig" a device once per game session
Giant Killer	V	+1d6 damage when attacking large creatures
Hard to Kill	N, WC, Sp d8	Ignore wound penalties for Vigor rolls made on the Knockout or Injury tables
Harder to Kill	V, Hard to Kill	50% chance of surviving "death"
Healer	N, Sp d8	+2 Healing
Hold the Line!	S, Sm d8, Command	Troops have +1 Toughness
Holy/Unholy Warrior	N, See text	See text
Inspire	S, Command	+1 to Spirit rolls of all troops in command
Investigator	N, Sm d8, Inv. d8, Streetwise d8	+2 Investigation and Streetwise
Jack-of-all-Trades	N, Sm d10	No −2 for unskilled Smarts based attempts

Edge	Requirements	Effect
Level Headed	S, Sm d8	Act on best of two cards in combat
Imp. Level Headed	S, Level Headed	Act on best of three cards in combat
Luck*	N	+1 benny per session
Great Luck*	N, Luck	+2 bennies per session
Marksman	S	Aim maneuver (+2 Shooting) if hero does not move
McGyver	N, Sm d6, Repair d6, Notice d8	May improvise temporary gadgets
Mentalist	N, AB (Psionics), Sm d8, Psionics d6	+2 to any opposed Psionics roll
Mighty Blow	WC, S, Fighting d10	Double melee damage when dealt Joker
Mr. Fix It	N, See text	+2 to Repair rolls, 1/2 Repair time with raise
Natural Leader	N, Sp d8, Command	Leader may give bennies to troops in command
Nerves of Steel	N, WC, V d8	Ignore 1 point of wound penalties
Imp. Nerves of Steel	N, Nerves of Steel	Ignore 2 points of wound penalties
New Power	N, AB	Character gains one new power
Noble*	N	Rich; +2 Charisma; Status and wealth
No Mercy	S	May spend bennies on damage rolls
Power Points	N, AB	+5 Power Points, once per rank only
Power Surge	WC, S, arcane skill d10	+2d6 Power Points when dealt a Joker
Professional	L, d12 in Trait	Trait becomes d12+1
Expert	L, Prof. in Trait	Trait becomes d12+2
Master	L, WC, Expert in Trait	Wild Die is d10 for one Trait
Quick*	N	Discard draw of 5 or less for new card
Quick Draw	N, A d8	May draw weapon as a free action
Rapid Recharge	S, Sp d6, AB	Regain 1 Power Point every 30 minutes
Imp. Rapid Recharge	V, Rapid Recharge	Regain 1 Power Point every 15 minutes
Rich*	N	3x starting funds, $75K annual salary
Filthy Rich*	N, Noble Birth or Rich	5x starting funds, $250K annual salary
Rock and Roll!	S, Shooting d8	Ignore full-auto penalty if shooter doesn't move
Scholar	N, d8 in affected skills	+2 to two different Knowledge skills
Sidekick	L, WC	Character gains a Novice WC sidekick
Soul Drain	S, See Text	Special
Steady Hands	N, A d8	Ignore unstable platform penalty
Sweep	N, St d8, Fighting d8	Attack all adjacent foes at −2
Imp. Sweep	V, Sweep	As above but with no penalty
Strong Willed	N, Intimidation d6, Taunt d6	+2 Intimidation and Taunt, +2 to resist
Thief	N, A d8, Climb d6, Lockpick d6, Stealth d8	+2 Climb, Lockpick, Stealth, or to disarm traps
Tough as Nails	L	Toughness +1
Imp. Tough as Nails	L, Tough as Nails	Toughness +2
Trademark Weapon	N, Fighting or Shooting d10	+1 Fighting or Shooting with particular weapon
Imp. Tr. Weapon	V, Trademark Weapon	+2 Fighting or Shooting with particular weapon
Two-Fisted	N, A d8	May attack with a weapon in each hand without multi-action penalty.
Weapon Master	L, Fighting d12	Parry +1
Master of Arms	L, Weapon Master	Parry +2
Wizard	N, See text	Each raise reduces cost of spell by 1 point
Woodsman	N, Sp d6, Survival d8, Tracking d8	+2 Tracking Survival, and Stealth

Background Edges—must be chosen during character creation.

Chapter Two: Gear

In the following section is a sampling of gear from the ancient era to the distant future. Below are some notes you'll need to understand the equipment lists.

AP (Armor Piercing): The weapon or round ignores this many points of Armor. A weapon with an AP value of 4, for instance, ignores 4 points of Armor. Excess AP is simply lost.

Armor: This is the amount of Armor provided by the equipment, which is added to the wearer's Toughness when the covered location is hit in combat. A character who wears multiple layers of armor only gains the highest bonus—they do not stack. Note that unless an attacker states otherwise, hits are always directed at the victim's torso.

Caliber: The number listed in parentheses after firearms is the caliber of bullet it fires. Use this when figuring ammunition costs or trying to figure out if the ammo from one weapon fits in another.

Cost: Equipment prices are relative both to the starting funds of $500 *and* to their tech level, so a Springfield musket doesn't really cost $250 in 1862. That's just the "worth" of the weapon relative to the tech level and the typical setting it's intended for. Remember that when comparing the $150 musket to the $150 AK47—the weapons are both "standard" for the typical environment they're found in, even though the AK is vastly superior to the musket. Characters in military campaigns shouldn't buy equipment at all—they're simply assigned their gear.

Economies are critical to balancing game worlds, so the Game Master is encouraged to re-price goods for his particular campaign.

Damage: Damage is listed in terms of dice. Projectile weapons have fixed damage (such as 2d6). Melee weapons have damage based on the wielder's Strength die plus another die, as listed under individual weapon entries. A dagger, for instance, inflicts Str+1d4 damage. (We'll discuss this in detail later on.)

A character whose Strength is lower than the weapon die can use the weapon, but there are penalties. First, the weapon die can't be higher than his Strength die. So if a scrawny kid (d4 Str) picks up a long sword (d8), he rolls 2d4 damage, not d4+d8. A brawny hero with Str d10 rolls d10+d8 when using the same long sword.

Second, if the Strength die isn't at least equal to the weapon die, the attacker doesn't get any of the weapon's inherent bonuses, such as +1 Parry or Reach. He still retains any penalties, however (like –1 Parry).

If a weapon has a damage listed as Str+d8+2, for instance, then the minimum Strength the wielder must have is a d8. The +2 or whatever, merely indicates the weapon is more lethal than other Str+d8 varieties (typically because it is magical or enhanced in some way).

Double Tap: The weapon can rapidly fire two rounds. Rather than rolling twice, add +1 to the Shooting and damage rolls.

Heavy Weapon: The weapon can affect vehicles or other devices with Heavy Armor.

HE (High Explosive): High explosive rounds use a burst template, the size of which is noted in the weapon or ammunition's notes. See the rules for Area of Effect attacks in the combat chapter.

Minimum Strength: Some ranged weapons list a minimum Strength to use. A character with a lower Strength can use the weapon, but suffers a −1 penalty to his attack roll for every step of difference between his Strength and the minimum Strength required. The penalty is ignored if the weapon can be braced on a bipod or other support.

Parry +X: The weapon adds the bonus to the character's Parry score when used.

Range: This lists the weapon's Short, Medium, and Long range. Ranges are listed in inches so that you can use a ruler to move, shoot, and fight on the table-top with miniatures. Each inch is equal to 2 yards in the real world, so that 5" is really 10 yards, or 30 feet.

Weapon ranges are "effective" ranges for the table-top. If you need to know the real world range of a weapon (for battles that don't take place on the table-top, for instance), multiply each range bracket by 2.5. A tank round with a Long range of 300, for example, has a "real world" Long range of 750", or 1500 yards.

Rate of Fire: This is the maximum number of shots that may be taken by this weapon per action. Unless a weapon says otherwise, the user can fire up to the weapon's Rate of Fire (rather than its full Rate of Fire). If a single shot is taken, it uses a single round of ammunition and does not incur any recoil penalties. Two or more shots with such weapons always incurs the −2 autofire penalty.

Reach: Weapons with "reach" allow their user to make Fighting attacks at the listed range. A reach of 1", for example, allows a character to strike a target 1" distant. Weapons without a reach value can only strike targets at arm's length (adjacent).

ENCUMBRANCE

A character can carry five times his Strength die type in pounds without incurring any penalties. This is called his "Load Limit." A character with a Strength of d8, for example, can comfortably carry 40 pounds. (Ignore normal clothes when figuring weight.)

Carrying too much weight inflicts a −1 penalty for every additional multiple of your Load Limit. The penalty applies to all Agility and Strength totals, as well as skills linked to either of those two attributes.

A hero with a d8 Strength, for example, has a Load Limit of 40 pounds. He can carry 41-80 pounds at a −1 penalty to his Strength, Agility, and related skill rolls. He could also carry 81-120 pounds at −2, or 121-160 pounds at −3.

Characters cannot regularly carry weight that inflicts a penalty of more than −3. They may be able to lift greater weights (up to a −4 penalty) for a few short steps at the discretion of the GM, however.

Reach can be very important when fighting from horseback and *against* mounted foes.

Reloading: Antique weapons, such as muskets and crossbows, are very slow to reload. Each weapon tells you how many actions it requires to reload.

Snapfire Penalty: Certain weapons, such as sniper rifles, are very inaccurate if fired "from the hip" rather than using their excellent sights or scopes. If the character moves in the action he fires, he suffers a –2 penalty.

Three Round Burst: The weapon can fire 3 rounds with one pull of the trigger. This adds +2 to the Shooting and damage rolls at the cost of the extra ammunition.

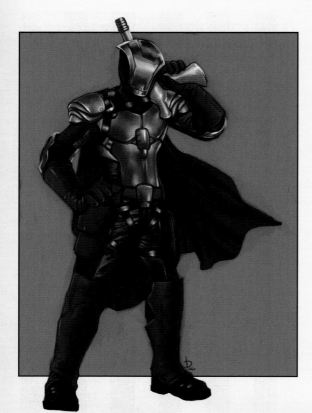

SELECTED GEAR NOTES

Below are some notes on some of the equipment listed in this chapter.

ARMOR

Note that the weights listed for most large suits of armor such as hauberks, plate, and power armor, are figured for their "distributed" weight. This assumes the armor is properly fitted, which takes a Knowledge (Armorsmithing) roll, some basic tools, and 1d6 hours. If armor is not properly fitted (such as when wearing armor taken from a foe), the weight is typically doubled.

KEVLAR

Kevlar offers 2 points of protection against most attacks. Kevlar weave "binds" spinning bullets and so negates up to 4 points of AP from bullets, and provides +4 protection from them as well.

POWER ARMOR

Power armor suits carry much of their own mass, hence the low weight values. Scout suits weigh 100 pounds when powered down, Battle suits weight 150, and Heavy Suits weigh 220 pounds. All power armor contains comm-units with a 5-mile range.

Powered armor typically lasts for one week without recharge. It requires a special recharging facility and 10 hours to return to full power. The GM may decide suits lose power faster under excessive use.

Scout Suit: These suits are made for reconnaissance. In addition to the standard comm-unit, they are coated in stealth paint that adds +4 to Stealth rolls vs radar and other automated detection systems (but not people).

Battle Suit: This the standard power armor worn by most heavy troopers in futuristic settings. It increases Strength by one die type, adds +2 to Pace, and allows users to jump 2d6" horizontally or 1d6" vertically. A Heads Up Display provides targeting information for linked weapons, adding +1 to the wearer's Shooting rolls.

Heavy Suit: Heavy suits (or assault suits) are designed for hard fighting under the most intense combat conditions. They subtract 2 from Pace and boost Strength by two die types. These suits mount at least one heavy weapon of some sort such as a flamethrower or a minigun, and feature enhanced targeting computers that add +2 to the character's Shooting rolls.

SHIELDS

If a character with a shield is hit by a ranged attack from the protected side, roll damage normally, but add the Armor bonus of the shield to the character's Toughness in the affected area (it acts as an obstacle).

RANGED WEAPONS & ACCESSORIES

BIPODS

Most full machine guns are also equipped with either an integral or detachable bipod. Once deployed, these provide a more stable shooting position and help control recoil.

It takes one action to deploy a bipod and set the weapon up. Once in position the autofire penalty is reduced to −1. If the hero moves, this benefit is negated and he will have to spend another action to redeploy the bipod.

SCOPES

Optical scopes can be attached to all manner of firearms from rifles to hand guns, and magnify targets to make distance shooting easier.

A scope provides a +2 Shooting bonus to shots over Short range as long as the firer does not move this round.

SHOTGUNS

Shotguns fire a spread of metal balls (also called "shot"), and so do more damage at close range where the spread is less and more of the shot hits the target. Farther away, the shot spreads more and causes less damage. Because of the increased chance of hitting someone due to the spread, shotguns add +2 to their user's Shooting rolls.

Shotguns do 1d6 damage at Long range, 2d6 at Medium, and 3d6 at Short range.

Double Barrels: Shotguns with two attached barrels are called "double barrels." If the attacker wants to fire both barrels at once, he makes a single Shooting roll. If the attack hits, roll damage for both shots.

Slugs: Shotguns can also fire slugs. The attacker doesn't get the +2 shotgun bonus to his Shooting roll, but the damage is 2d10 regardless of the range increment.

SPECIAL WEAPONS

Note that special weapons don't have a cost, as most are only available to military organizations. Those listed with a **Cost** of "Military" are generally not available on the open market, but are provided by governments to their armed forces.

BOUNCING BETTIES

These deadly mines are designed to pop up into the air and rain shrapnel down from about head-height. Only full overhead cover offers an Armor bonus against such devices. Simply being prone offers no protection from these deadly explosives.

CANNONS

Cannons can fire three different types of shells: solid shot, shrapnel, and canister. The crew can pick the type of ammunition to be loaded each time it reloads.

Solid Shot is just that—big round balls made to batter walls or plow through packed ranks of troops. To fire, the leader of the crew makes a Shooting roll as usual. A target directly behind and adjacent to the first is also hit on a d6 roll of 1-3, and takes full damage. This continues until there are no more adjacent foes.

Shrapnel is an explosive shell filled with metal balls, nails, and other scraps. The debris is hurled outward when the shell explodes, shredding lightly armored targets in a shower of steel. Shrapnel is an area effect attack, and uses the Medium Burst Template.

Canister is a shell made to detonate inside the barrel of the cannon. The jagged metal inside the "canister" then sprays out of the cannon to shred anything within its deadly cone like a giant shotgun. To determine the effects of canister, place a ruler in front of the cannon in the direction you want it to fire and make a Shooting roll with no range modifiers. If the shot is missed, move the far end of the ruler 1" left or right (roll randomly).

Now place a Medium Burst Template at the near end of the ruler and move it directly forward along that path for 24". Every target under the template is hit for 2d6 damage. Cover acts as Armor just as with any area effect weapon, meaning prone characters add +2 to their Toughness.

Reloading: Cannons require one action to reload with a crew of four, or two actions with less crewmen.

Line of Sight: Cannon crews must be able to see their targets to hit them. Howitzers, mortars, and bombards may fire at targets they cannot see (assuming they know roughly where the target is) at a –4 penalty, and double deviation (see **Combat**).

Flamethrowers

Flamethrowers include any device that squirts an incendiary liquid or even pure flame. To use it, the attacker places the small end of the Cone Template at the tip of his character's weapon, and the large end on as many targets as he's able. The attacker then makes a Shooting roll at +2. Defenders who make an Agility roll equal to or greater than the attacker's Shooting total move out of the way and are unaffected. The rest suffer the weapon's damage (typically 2d10) and roll to see if they catch fire (see **Fire**).

Raises on the attacker's Shooting roll have no additional effect—targets are flamed or not.

Vehicular Flamethrowers: Military organizations often have flamethrowers with much longer ranges. The flame fired from a British Crocodile, for example, has a range of about 70 yards (35"). The flame must be arced to reach these distances however, so a character may choose to use a Small Burst Template instead of the Cone Template when using such weapons. The center of the template may be placed up to the maximum range of the particular flamethrower, as listed in its notes. This is treated just like any other area effect attack, though targets still get a chance to dodge out.

Grenades

Grenades work as usual, but a character within the burst radius has two additional options. To pick up and throw the grenade before it goes off, he must make an

Agility roll at –4 (or –2 if he was on Hold). Failure means it goes off and he takes an additional die of damage.

Covering Grenades: A character may also throw himself on a grenade. He takes double the normal dice of damage for his heroic act, but his total Toughness is subtracted from the damage inflicted on other characters in the blast radius.

Allies won't normally perform such a suicidal act, though the GM might rule otherwise in specific situations, such as when an ally has a "loyal" personality.

MISSILES

Air-to-air (or space-to-space) weapons are designed to destroy enemy fighters and other small targets with a focused warhead. To activate, the pilot must first "capture" the target's signature on his own control panel. This is accomplished by various means, including heat-signature, radar, emissions, or even profile, depending on tech level.

To get a lock, the pilot picks his target and must then succeed at an opposed Piloting roll. The attacker must subtract range modifiers from the Piloting roll just as if he were Shooting.

Once locked, the pilot then how many missiles to release (usually up to his full payload depending on his craft). At Short Range, the target has one round to evade. He has two rounds (and chances) at Medium Range, and three at Long Range.

Evading a missile requires a Piloting roll at –4. Note that many craft contain additional evasion systems, such as chaff or flares, that add to this roll.

Anti-Missile Systems: Larger ships often have anti-missile systems designed to shoot down missiles with targeted lasers, walls of matter, or hails of lead. All systems require a modicum of skill and a lot of luck. First the crewman in charge of the particular AMS battery makes a Shooting roll minus the range. (Don't subtract for the size or speed of the missile—the AMS already accounts for that.) Each successful hit has a 1 in 6 chance of shooting down the torpedo. A Phalanx system with a RoF of 6, for example, rolls 6 dice, and each hit gives the defender a 1 in 6 chance of shooting the torpedo down.

Obstacles: Evading prey can add +2 to the Piloting roll with substantial cover—such as asteroids, canyon walls, or the hull of a capital ship.

ARMOR

MEDIEVAL ARMOR

Type	Armor	Weight*	Cost	Notes
Personal				
Leather	+1	15	50	Covers torso, arms, legs
Chain hauberk (long coat)	+2	25	300	Covers torso, arms, legs
Plate corselet	+3	25	400	Covers torso
Plate arms (vambace)	+3	10	200	Covers arms
Plate leggings (greaves)	+3	15	300	Covers legs
Pot Helm	+3	4	75	50% vs head shot
Steel Helmet (enclosed)	+3	8	150	Covers head
Barding				
Plate barding	+3	30	1250	For horses
Shields **				
Small Shield (Buckler)	—	8	25	+1 Parry
Medium Shield	—	12	50	+1 Parry, +2 Armor to ranged shots that hit
Large Shield (Kite, Pavise)	—	20	200	+2 Parry, +2 Armor to ranged shots that hit

**Shields protect only against attacks from the front and left (assuming a right-handed character).*

MODERN ARMOR

Type	Armor	Weight*	Cost	Notes
Flak Jacket	+2/+4	12	80	Covers torso
Kevlar Vest	+2/+4	8	250	Covers torso only, negates 4 AP, see notes
Kevlar Vest w/inserts	+4/+8	12	2500	As Kevlar, but ceramic inserts are +8 vs. bullets
Motorcycle helmet	+3	5	75	50% chance vs head shot
Steel Pot (helmet)	+4	5	80	50% chance vs head shot

FUTURISTIC ARMOR

Type	Armor	Weight*	Cost	Notes
Infantry Battle Suit	+6	20	Mil	Covers entire body, near-future military, bomb suit
Hard Armor	+8	30	Mil	Covers entire body, future military
Powered Armor (Scout Suit)	+10	0	Mil	Covers entire body, far future military
Powered Armor (Battle Suit)	+12	0	Mil	Covers entire body, far future military
Powered Armor (Heavy Suit)	+14	0	Mil	Covers entire body, far future military
Reflective Vest	+10	5	200	Covers torso, far future, works against lasers only

This is effective weight when worn. Most armor weighs quite a bit more when carried rather than worn.

HAND WEAPONS

MEDIEVAL

Type	Damage	Weight	Cost	Notes
Blades				
Dagger	Str+d4	1	25	
Great sword	Str+d10	12	400	Parry −1, 2 hands
Flail	Str+d6	8	200	Ignores Shield Parry and Cover bonus
Katana	Str+d6+2	6	1000	AP 2
Long sword	Str+d8	8	300	Includes scimitars
Rapier	Str+d4	3	150	Parry +1
Short sword	Str+d6	4	200	Includes cavalry sabers
Axes and Mauls				
Axe	Str+d6	2	200	
Battle Axe	Str+d8	10	300	
Great Axe	Str+d10	15	500	AP 1, Parry −1, 2 hands
Maul	Str+d8	20	400	AP 2 vs. rigid armor, Parry −1, 2 hands
Warhammer	Str+d6	8	250	AP 1 vs. rigid armor (plate mail)
Pole Arms				
Halberd	Str+d8	15	250	Reach 1, 2 hands
Lance	Str+d8	10	300	AP 2 when charging, Reach 2
Pike	Str+d8	25	400	Reach 2, requires 2 hands
Staff	Str+d4	8	10	Parry +1, Reach 1, 2 hands
Spear	Str+d6	5	100	Parry +1, Reach 1, 2 hands

MODERN

Type	Damage	Weight	Cost	Notes
Bangstick	3d6	2	5	Must be reloaded (1 action)
Bayonet	Str+d4	1	25	A bayonet affixed to a rifle increases the damage to Str+d6, Parry +1, Reach 1, 2 hands
Billy club/Baton	Str+d4	1	10	Carried by most law-enforcement officials
Brass knuckles	Str+d4	1	20	A hero wearing brass knuckles is considered to be an Unarmed Attacker
Chainsaw	2d6+4	20	200	A natural 1 on the Fighting die (regardless of the Wild Die) hits the user instead
Switchblade	Str+d4	1	10	−2 to be Noticed if hidden
Survival knife	Str+d4	3	50	Contains supplies that add +1 to Survival rolls

FUTURISTIC

Type	Damage	Weight	Cost	Notes
Molecular knife	Str+d4+2	1	250	AP 2, Cannot be thrown
Molecular sword	Str+d8+2	8	500	AP 4
Laser sword	Str+d6+8	5	1000	AP 12, Laser swords aren't terribly realistic, but are staples in many space-opera campaigns

MEDIEVAL

Type	Range	Damage	RoF	Cost	Weight	Shots	Min Str.	Notes
Axe, throwing	3/6/12	Str+d6	1	75	2	—	-	
Bow	12/24/48	2d6	1	250	3	—	d6	
Crossbow	15/30/60	2d6	1	500	10	—	d6	AP 2, 1 action to reload
English Long Bow	15/30/60	2d6	1	200	5	—	d8	
Knife/Dagger	3/6/12	Str+d4	1	25	1	—	-	
Sling	4/8/16	Str+d4	1	10	1	—	-	
Spear	3/6/12	Str+d6	1	100	5	—	d6	

BLACK POWDER

Type	Range	Damage	RoF	Cost	Weight	Shots	Min Str	Notes
Brown Bess (.75)	10/20/40	2d8	1	300	15	—	d6	2 actions to reload
Blunderbuss (8G)	10/20/40	1-3d6*	1	300	12	—	d6	2 actions to reload
Flintlock Pistol (.60)	5/10/20	2d6+1	1	150	3	—	—	2 actions to reload
Kentucky Rifle (.45)	15/30/60	2d8	1	300	8	—	d6	AP 2, 3 actions to reload
Springfield (.52)	15/30/60	2d8	1	250	11	—	d6	2 actions to reload

A blunderbuss does 1d6 at Long range, 2d6 at Medium range, and 3d6 at Close range.

MODERN

Type	Range	Damage	RoF	Cost	Weight	Shots	Min Str	Notes
Pistols								
Derringer (.44)	5/10/20	2d6+1	1	150	2	2	—	AP 1
Colt Dragoon (.44)	12/24/48	2d6+1	1	200	4	6	—	Revolver
Colt 1911 (.45)	12/24/48	2d6+1	1	200	4	7	—	AP 1, Semi-Auto
S&W (.44)	12/24/48	2d6+1	1	250	5	6	—	AP 1, Revolver
Desert Eagle (.50)	15/30/60	2d8	1	300	8	7	—	AP 2, Semi-Auto
Glock (9mm)	12/24/48	2d6	1	200	3	17	—	AP 1, Semi-Auto
Peacemaker (.45)	12/24/48	2d6+1	1	200	3	6	—	AP 1, Revolver
Ruger (.22)	10/20/40	2d6-1	1	100	2	9	—	Semi-Auto
S&W (.357)	12/24/48	2d6+1	1	250	4	6	—	AP 1, Revolver
Submachine Guns								
H&K MP5 (9mm)	12/24/48	2d6	3	300	10	30	—	AP 1, Auto
MP40 (9mm)	12/24/48	2d6	3	300	11	32	—	AP 1, Auto

Type	Range	Damage	RoF	Cost	Weight	Shots	Min Str	Notes
Tommy Gun (.45)	12/24/48	2d6+1	3	350	13	50	—	AP 1, Auto
Uzi (9mm)	12/24/48	2d6	3	300	9	32	—	AP 1, Auto

Shotguns

Type	Range	Damage	RoF	Cost	Weight	Shots	Min Str	Notes
Double-Barrel (12g)	12/24/48	1-3d6	1-2	150	11	2	—	See notes
Pump Action (12g)	12/24/48	1-3d6	1	150	8	6	—	See notes
Sawed-Off DB (12g)	5/10/20	1-3d6	1-2	150	6	2	—	See notes
Streetsweeper (12g)	12/24/48	1-3d6	1	450	10	12	—	See notes

Rifles

Type	Range	Damage	RoF	Cost	Weight	Shots	Min Str	Notes
Barrett (.50)	50/100/200	2d10	1	750	35	11	d8	AP 4, Snapfire, HW
M1 (.30)	24/48/96	2d8	1	300	10	8	d6	AP 2, Semi-Auto
Kar98 (7.92)	24/48/96	2d8	1	300	9	5	d6	AP 2
Sharps Big 50 (.50)	30/60/120	2d10	1	400	11	1	d8	AP 2, Snapfire Penalty
Spencer Carbine (.52)	20/40/80	2d8	1	250	8	7	—	AP 2
Winchester '76 (.45-.47)	24/48/96	2d8	1	300	10	15	d6	AP 2, uses special .45-.47 long cartridges

Assault Rifles

Type	Range	Damage	RoF	Cost	Weight	Shots	Min Str	Notes
AK47 (7.62)	24/48/96	2d8+1	3	450	10	30	d6	AP 2, Auto
H&K G3 (.308)	24/48/96	2d8	3	400	10	20	d6	AP 2, Auto
M-16 (5.56)	24/48/96	2d8	3	400	8	20 or 30	—	AP 2, Auto, 3RB
Steyr AUG (5.56)	24/48/96	2d8	3	400	8	30	—	AP 2, Auto, 3RB

Machine Guns

Type	Range	Damage	RoF	Cost	Weight	Shots	Min Str	Notes
Gatling (.45)	24/48/96	2d8	3	500	40	100	—	AP 2, May not move
M2 Browning (.50)	50/100/200	2d10	3	1000	84	200	—	AP 4, May not move, HW
M1919 (.30)	24/48/96	2d8	3	750	32	250	—	AP 2, May not move
M60 (7.62)	30/60/120	2d8+1	3	1000	33	250	d8	AP 2, Snapfire
MG42 (7.92)	30/60/120	2d8+1	4	500	26	200	d8	AP 2, Snapfire
SAW (5.56)	30/60/120	2d8	4	750	20	200	d8	AP 2, Snapfire

FUTURISTIC

Type	Range	Damage*	RoF	Cost	Weight	Shots	Min Str	Notes
Laser Pistol	15/30/60	1-3d6	1	200	4	24	—	Semi-Auto
Laser Rifle	30/60/120	1-3d6	3	300	8	48	d6	Auto, 3RB
Laser MG	50/100/200	1-3d6	5	500	15	200	d8	Auto

*Increasing the damage per attack uses a like number of shots. A 3d6 attack, for instance, uses up 3 shots. Semi-Auto: May Double Tap. Auto: Fully Automatic or Single Shot. 3RB: Has a 3-round burst selector. HW= Heavy Weapon

Mundane Items

Item	Cost*	Weight
Adventuring Gear		
Backpack	50	2
Bedroll (sleeping bag; winterized)	25	4
Blanket	10	4
Camera (disposable)	10	1
Camera (regular)	75	2
Camera (digital)	300	1
Candle (provides light in 2" radius)	1	1
Canteen (waterskin)	5	1
Cellular Phone	100	-
Crowbar	10	2
Flashlight (10" beam)	20	3
Flask (ceramic)	5	1
Flint and steel	3	1
Grappling hook	100	2
Hammer	10	1
Lantern (provides light in 4" radius)	25	3
Lighter	2	-
Lockpicks	200	1
Handcuffs (manacles)	15	2
Oil (for lantern; 1 pint)	2	1
Quiver (holds 20 arrows / bolts)	25	2
Rope (10")	10	15
Shovel	5	5
Soap	1	1/5
Tool Kit	200	5
Torch (1 hour, 4" radius)	5	1
Umbrella	5	2
Whistle	2	—
Whetstone	5	1
Clothing		
Camouflage Fatigues	20	-
Hiking Boots	100	-
Normal clothing	20	—
Formal clothing	200	—
Winter gear (cloak / parka)	200	3
Winter boots	100	1

Item	Cost*	Weight
Food		
Fast Food meal (cheap meal)	5	1
Good meal (restaurant)	15+	—
MRE (Meal Ready to Eat)	10	1
Trail rations (5 meals; keeps 1 week)	10	5
Animals & Tack		
Horse	300	—
War Horse	750	—
Saddle	10	10
Elaborate saddle	50	10
War Horse barding (+3)	1250	30
Computers		
Desktop	800	20
Laptop	1200	5
Handheld	250	1
GPS	250	1
Surveillance		
Cellular Interceptor	650	5
Lineman's Telephone (Repair roll to tap into a phone line)	150	2
Night Vision Goggles		
Passive (no penalties for Dim or Dark)	1000	3
Active (no penalties for any level of darkness)	2500	4
Parabolic Microphone (good to 200 yards)	750	4
Telephone Tap (Bug)	250	-
Transmitter Detector	525	1

Costs for mundane items depend entirely on the setting and the tech level available. A horse in most fantasy campaigns, for instance, is fairly common and costs about $300. In the modern world, horses cost thousands of dollars.

SPECIAL WEAPONS

Type	Range	Damage	RoF	Cost	Min Str	Notes
Cannon (shot)	50/100/200	3d6+1	1	Military	—	AP 4, See notes, HW
Shrapnel shell	50/100/200	3d6	1	—	—	Medium Burst Template
Canister	24" path	2d6	1	—	—	See notes
Rocket Launchers						
Bazooka	24/48/96	4d8	1	Military	—	Med Burst Template, AP 9, Snapfire, HW
Panzershrek	15/30/60	4d8	1	—	—	Med Burst Template, AP 17, Snapfire, HW
Panzerfaust	12/24/48	4d8	1	—	—	Med Burst Template, AP 20, Snapfire, HW
M203 40MM	24/48/96	4d8	1	—	—	Med Burst Template, Snapfire
M72 Law	24/48/96	4d8+2	1	—	—	Med Burst Template, AP 30, Snapfire, HW
AT-4	24/48/96	4d8+2	1	—	—	Med Burst Template, AP 40, Snapfire, HW
Mines						
Anti-Personnel Mine	—	2d6+2	—	Military	—	Small Burst Template
Anti-Tank Mine	—	4d6	—	Military	—	Med Burst Template, AP 5 against half weakest
Bouncing Betty	—	3d6	—	Military	—	Small Burst Template, see notes
Claymore Mine	—	3d6	—	Military	—	Treat as canister
Flamethrowers						
Flamethrower	Cone Template	2d10	1	Military	d6	Ignores Armor
Grenade						
Mk67 Pineapple (US)	5/10/20*	3d6	—	75	—	Med Burst Template
Potato Masher (Ger)	5/10/20*	3d6-2	—	50	—	Med Burst Template

AMMUNITION

Ammo	Weight	Cost	Notes
Arrow*	1/5	1/2	—
Man-Killer Arrow	1/5	1	+1 damage, usually found only in Oriental settings
Teflon Arrow	1/5	5	AP 2, modern eras only
Bullets, small	3/50	10/50	Includes .22 to .32 caliber weapons
Bullets, medium	5/50	25/50	Includes 9mm to .45
Bullets, large	8/50	50/50	Includes .50 and most rifle rounds
Quarrel*	1/5	2	AP 2 (standard crossbow bolt)
Laser battery	1	25	Provides one full load of shots for the laser pistol, rifle, or MG
Shot (w/powder)	1/10	3	For black powder weapons
Sling stone	1/10	1/20	Stones can also be found for free with a Notice roll and 1d10 minutes searching, depending on terrain

*Outdoors, arrows and quarrels are recovered on a d6 roll of 4-6 (50% chance). Underground or indoors, the chance is reduced to a roll of 5-6 on 1d6 to reflect the increased chance of breakage.

Vehicle Notes

The following pages include information on some select vehicles for land, air, and even the water. They're grouped by type to help you when purchasing or choosing equipment.

Acc/Top Speed is the vehicle's Acceleration and Top Speed in inches per round. The Top Speed of vehicles is set for battlefields (not the open highway, where they can usually double their speed). More importantly, they're adapted to work well on the table-top. This means they're not entirely realistic, but work well for the game.

Climb is how many inches an aircraft can climb each round. See the **Vehicle Rules** for more details.

Toughness is the vehicle's base durability Armor, which is already figured in to its Toughness (in parentheses).

Passengers lists the number of crew plus any additional passengers it can transport.

Cost is the average price of the vehicle.

Special Notes

Air Bags: Roll half the normal damage dice in a collision (round down), minus one additional die when rolling for passenger's damage from collisions.

Amphibious: The vehicle can enter water without flooding or capsizing. See the individual descriptions for their movement rates while in water.

AMCM (Anti-Missile Counter Measures): Some jets or spacecraft are equipped with anti-missile counter measures, such as chaff, flares, or decoy pods. The number of AMCM is a reflection of "bursts," not actual flares or decoys. When used, an AMCM adds +2 to the user's Piloting roll *that round only* for purposes of evading missiles.

Fixed Gun: The vehicle's weapon cannot rotate.

Four Wheel Drive: These vehicles treat each inch of difficult terrain as 1.5 (instead of 2).

Heavy Armor: Only weapons marked as Heavy Weapons can hurt this vehicle, regardless of the damage roll. This keeps a really lucky pistol shot from destroying a King Tiger. Vehicles with Heavy Armor halve damage they take from colliding with other obstacles (including vehicles) that don't have Heavy Armor.

Heavy Weapon: This weapon can harm vehicles equipped with Heavy Armor.

Improved Stabilizer: These computerized compensation systems eliminate the moving vehicle penalty when firing vehicle-mounted weapons altogether.

Infrared Night Vision: Thermal imaging devices halve darkness penalties (round down) for heat-producing targets.

Night Vision: "Starlight" and other night vision equipment eliminate Dim and Dark lighting penalties.

Sloped Armor: In the best armored vehicles, armor is sloped so as to increase the chance that a hit will be deflected off the tank's armor. The number after the Sloped Armor ability is the penalty to the attack roll of anyone firing on the vehicle.

Spacecraft: The vehicle is designed for use in outer space. Those followed with /Atmospheric can enter and exit planetary orbits as well.

Stealth Paint: This is black paint that imposes a –4 to rolls made to spot the vehicle with sensors.

Stabilizer: A stabilizer reduces the penalty for firing a specific weapon from a moving vehicle to –1.

Tracked: Unless otherwise noted, the vehicle is assumed to have wheels. Tracked vehicles can climb over most low obstacles such as logs, and treat each inch of difficult terrain as 1.5 (instead of 2).

Weapons: Weapons are statted in the vehicle's text. Note that the Rate of Fire for missiles and rockets indicates how many may be fired in one attack.

VEHICLES

Vehicle	Acc/TS	Toughness	Crew	Cost	Notes
Horse & Carriage	*	10 (2)	1+3	$1-3K	See horse statistics
Early Car	5/16	8 (2)	1+3	$1000	Model Ts and the like
Motorcycle	20/36	8 (2)	1+1	$3000	Street bike
Dirt Bike	15/32	8 (2)	1	$2000	+4 Toughness vs jumps; Off Road (4WD)
Compact Car	10/36	10 (3)	1+3	$5-14K	Neons, Chevettes
Mid-Sized Car	20/40	11 (3)	1+4	$20-60K	Air bags, luxury features
SUV	20/40	14 (3)	1+7	$20-60K	Luxury features; 4WD
Sports Car	30/56	10 (3)	1+3	$15-$300K	Mustang to Lamborghini
Semi	5/30	16 (4)	1+1	$150-300K	Trailer is Toughness 14 (2)
Aircraft					
Helicopter	20/50	11 (2)	1+3	$500K+	Climb 20
Cessna Skyhawk	20/48	12 (2)	1+3	$150K+	Climb 10
Learjet	25/200	14 (2)	2+10	$20M+	Climb 25
Civilian Space Shuttle	70/800	16 (4)	1+40	$250K+	Climb 75
Watercraft					
Rowboat	1/2	8 (2)	1+3	$500	—
Cigarette Boat	20/40	10 (2)	1+3	$60K+	—
Small Yacht	2/10	13 (2)	1+9	$500K+	—
Hydrofoil	4/13	15 (3)	1+9	$400K+	Can sport various armaments
Galleon	2/6	20 (4)	20+80	$300K+	46 cannon; Heavy armor
Galley	2/8	19 (4)	20+100	$150K	Acc/TS 1/3 under sail; small catapult (Range 24/48/96; Damage 3d6; RoF 1; AP 4; SBT; Heavy Weapon)

Chapter Three: Game Rules

It's time to learn how to actually play the game. Don't worry—it's not hard! You'll be ready to go in no time!

Wild Cards & Extras

Your hero (a player character), and unique villains and monsters are collectively called "Wild Cards." These beings have a little better chance at doing things, are a little tougher to put down, and are generally more detailed than common guards, minions, or lackeys—collectively called "Extras."

Wild Cards are noted with the picture of Smiling Jack by their name, like this:

Buck Savage

Besides your own characters, it's up to the Game Master to decide which NPCs are Wild Cards. The sergeant of the City Watch probably isn't a Wild Card, but Sergeant Grimlock of the City Watch, a veteran of many wars and an important character in your campaign, certainly is. Skytch the Dragon is also a Wild Card, though his three young wyrms aren't. You'll see the difference between Wild Cards and Extras as you continue to read, but for later reference, the differences are:

• Wild Cards suffer multiple wounds.
• Wild Cards always roll a Wild Die along with their Trait die when making tests and take the better of the two.

Trait Tests

To use an attribute or skill, simply roll the die assigned to it. If the result is a 4 or better (the "Target Number" or TN), you're successful!

Modifiers

Circumstances modify your die roll, such as shooting at something at long range or finding a well-hidden clue. Some things, such as ranged attacks, have standard modifiers. It's up to the GM to determine any modifiers for more subjective tasks, such as spotting an ambush or eavesdropping on a conversation through a door.

In general, an easy task, such as finding tracks in the mud, is made at +2. A difficult task, such as finding tracks by torchlight, is made at −2. A very difficult task, such as finding tracks in a rainstorm, is made at −4.

The Wild Die

Extras roll a single die as described above. But Wild Cards roll an extra d6 and take the highest of their normal die or the "Wild Die" when making skill or attribute rolls. Wild Dice are rolled just like the Trait die, and can Ace as well (see below).

The downside is that snake-eyes (double 1s) on one of these rolls is a critical failure of some sort. The GM gets to make up something rotten to happen to your character. That's the price Fate charges for making someone a hero.

Unskilled Attempts

If a character doesn't have a skill for an action he's attempting, he rolls 1d4 and subtracts 2 from the total. Wild Card characters still get their Wild Die for these rolls (which are also subject to the −2 penalty). The GM may occasionally decide that a character has no chance at a particular skill if he has no training in it—such as performing surgery or flying a plane.

ACES

All Trait tests and damage rolls in *Savage Worlds* are "open-ended." That means that when you roll the highest number possible on a die (a 6 on a d6, an 8 on a d8, and so on), you get to roll that die again and add it to the total. This is called an "Ace." Any modifiers to the die roll should be tacked on after adding up an Aced roll.

Example: Buck Savage, an international adventurer, is fighting a group of wild-eyed cultists. He has a d10 Shooting and rolls an Ace (a 10), and so rolls again. He gets another 10, then rolls again and gets a 3. His total is (10+10+3=) 23!

OPPOSED ROLLS

Sometimes rolls are "opposed" by an opponent. If two characters are wrestling for control of an ancient artifact, for example, they both make Strength rolls and compare results.

When this happens, the acting character gets his Trait total first. If he wants to spend bennies (see the next section), he does so now. When he's satisfied with his total, his opponent gets to roll. The highest total wins. In a tie, the two foes continue to struggle with no clear victor.

RAISES

Sometimes it's important to know just how successful a Trait test was. Every 4 points over what you need for success is called a "raise." If your hero needs a 4 to Shoot an opponent and rolls an 11, he hits with one raise (and would have two raises with a roll of 12). Figure raises after adjusting for any modifiers.

COOPERATIVE ROLLS

Sometimes characters may want to cooperate and help a friend complete some kind of urgent task. If two or more characters want to perform a task together (and the GM decides it's possible for them to do so), the lead character makes his roll and adds +1 for every success and raise his companions achieved on their own rolls. This has a normal maximum of +4 for all tasks except those of Strength, which have no maximum.

Example: Buck and Virginia research the Eye of Kilquato together. The GM decides that's reasonable. Buck is the lead character and makes his Investigation roll. Virginia makes a roll as well and gets a raise. She adds +2 to Buck's total.

GROUP ROLLS

When you want to make a noncombat Trait roll for a group of Extras you don't have to roll it one character at a time, instead roll one Trait die as usual along with a Wild Die. Take the best of the two as always and treat this as the group's total. This way you get a nice average without having to make Guts rolls for every NPC who sees a dragon, or watch one goofball ruin a stealthy approach for his 49 companions.

If you roll a 5, for example, and a benny gets you a 4, keep the original 5 instead.

Bennies cannot be spent on tables, damage rolls (unless a character has the No Mercy Edge), or any other roll that isn't a Trait roll.

Soak Rolls

Bennies can also be used to save your bacon from deadly attacks. Choose carefully where you spend them! See **Damage** for complete information on how to make Soak rolls.

Game Master Bennies

Game Masters get bennies too. At the start of each session, the GM gets one benny for each player character. He may use these for any of his villains throughout the course of the night.

Each of the GM's Wild Cards also gets two bennies per game session. They can use these or any of the bennies in the "common" pool to save their evil skins, but they can't share their own bennies with other nonplayer characters.

As with heroes, bennies are not saved between sessions.

Example: A vile crocodile cult is led by an evil shaman (a Wild Card). Buck and Virginia are the only player characters, so the GM gets two bennies for the shaman, plus two more for the pair of player characters.

The shaman can use any of the bennies, but his fanatical tribesmen, crocodile servants, and other minions can only use the two from the common pool.

Bennies

Every now and then the dice may betray you. That's why *Savage Worlds* gives you, the player, a little control over your hero's fate.

Every player starts each game session with three "bennies," gaming stones or other tokens that signify a little bit of good luck or fate. The Game Master may also give you more bennies for great roleplaying, overcoming major obstacles, or even entertaining everyone with an outlandish action, side-splitting in-game joke, or other memorable act. (Tips for awarding bennies can be found under Advancement.)

You can use bennies to reroll any Trait test. Make the entire roll from scratch. If you're firing three shots on full-auto and don't like the results, pick up all three dice and your Wild Die and roll again. You can keep spending bennies and rerolling as long as you like, and take the best of your attempts.

COMBAT

Great heroes must often overcome violent foes. Here's how to resolve fights in *Savage Worlds.*

TIME

When a fight breaks out, game time breaks down into rounds of six seconds each. Ten rounds, then, is one minute.

THE BATTLEFIELD

In combat with more than a few opponents, the Game Master should make a quick map of the terrain on some sort of erasable surface. Chessex® makes great Battle Mats™ already marked off with 1" squares or hexes (visit them at www.chessex.com).

You can then place miniatures on the map to show exactly where everyone is during the fight.

The terrain can be sketched out quickly and easily with an erasable marker to make sure everyone understands the tactical situation. You can also use miniatures terrain or a plain tabletop with a ruler. The more detailed you get, the more likely everyone is to make use of their surroundings and do more than just say "I attack."

DISTANCE

Movement, weapon ranges, and the like are listed in inches to help when playing with miniatures. In the "real world," each inch is equal to 2 yards.

If the GM needs a different scale to accommodate a larger battle, simply divide weapon and movement ranges as needed.

ALLIES

Allied NPCs are divided up among all the players to control. This is a very important part of *Savage Worlds* because our settings often feature allied bands of skilled hirelings, fellow grunts, or loyal retainers, and the game is designed to handle them quickly and easily. It's also designed for the *players* to control them—not the Game Master.

It doesn't matter whether or not the *characters* control the allies, only that the *players* do. This keeps everyone involved in the action even if his hero is out of the fight, and makes running large combats much easier and fun for everyone. Of course the GM can always take charge of NPCs when the need arises, but with good, mature roleplayers, this should rarely be necessary.

INITIATIVE

The action in *Savage Worlds* is fast and furious. To help the Game Master keep track of who goes in what order and add a little randomness, we use a single deck of playing cards with both Jokers left in to determine everyone's initiative.

Deal in characters as follows:
• Every Wild Card is dealt a single card. Any allies under that player's control act on his initiative card as well.
• Each group of Game Master characters, such as all zombies, all wolves, and so on, share a card.

Exactly which nonplayer character groups get their own cards is up to the GM. If he wants to break his 30 zombies into 5 groups of 6, that's fine. Your goal is to do whatever makes running the battle as quick and easy as possible. Generally, Wild Cards and other unique characters get their own card.

SHUFFLE

Shuffle the deck after any round in which a Joker was dealt (see below).

THE COUNTDOWN

Once the cards are dealt, the Game Master starts the round by counting down from the Ace to the Deuce, with each group resolving its actions when its card comes up.

Ties: Ties are resolved by suit order: Spades are first, then Hearts, Diamonds, and Clubs (reverse alphabetical order).

THE JOKER IS WILD!

What happens if you're dealt a Joker? Glad you asked. Jokers act as "wild cards." You can go whenever you want in the round, even interrupting another character's action if you want! In addition, you add +2 to all Trait tests this round, and +2 to damage totals as well!

Hold

A hero may choose to wait and see what happens by taking a Hold action. He may then go later in the round if he chooses. A Held action lasts until it's used. If a character has a Held card when a new round starts, he's not dealt in.

Interrupting Actions: If a character on Hold wants to interrupt an action, he and the opponent make opposed Agility rolls. Whoever rolls highest goes first. In the rare case of a tie, the actions are simultaneous.

Surprise

Combat often starts before everyone involved is prepared. An ambush, a sudden double-cross, or a trap might all give one side in a fight an edge over the other.

When this happens, the side that started the fight is not dealt cards, but begins the fight on Hold. Victims of the surprise attack must make Notice rolls. Those who make it are dealt in as usual. Those who fail get no card in the first round of combat.

> *Example: Buck and Virginia are creeping down the bank of a river when they're spotted by two native warriors hiding behind a tree. The natives wait until the two are within striking range to spring their attack.*
>
> *The two warriors are on Hold and get to attack immediately. If Buck and Virginia make their Notice rolls they're dealt in normally. If not, they have to wait until the next round to act.*

Standoff!

Occasionally, you might run into a situation where everyone is effectively on Hold. Maybe you're in the middle of a tense negotiation when one person goes for his gun. In these situations, everyone should roll their Agility since they are all on Hold and act in order of highest to lowest (ties are simultaneous). Deal everyone in as normal on the next round.

Actions

Characters perform "actions" when their card comes up each round. A character can perform one regular action—attacking, running, casting a spell, and so on—without penalty.

Multiple Actions

Characters may also perform multiple actions such as Intimidating someone while blasting away with a shotgun, running and Fighting, attacking with a weapon in each hand, and so on. A hero can't fire more than his weapon's rate of fire in a round, however, nor may he make more than one Fighting attack with the same weapon.

In essence, a hero may not perform the same action twice in a round. The actions are assumed to take place almost simultaneously, so a character couldn't make two simultaneous Intimidation rolls or cast two different spells. He could make a Fighting and a Shooting attack if he had a gun in one hand and a knife in the other, however, and could even issue a Taunt at the same time. He could only make two Fighting attacks if he had a knife in each hand, however (or had the Frenzy Edge).

Each additional action attempted in a round subtracts 2 from all the hero's rolls. If an adventurer wants to fire a gun with one hand and slice at an adjacent foe with the other, for instance, he subtracts 2 from both rolls. If he also wanted to make a test of wills against someone at the same time, he subtracts 4 from all his rolls.

Wild Cards get their Wild Die on each action as usual.

> *Example: Backed into a corner, Buck tries to shoot one cultist and Intimidate another. Both his Shooting and Intimidate totals suffer a −2 penalty because he took two actions instead of one.*

Free Actions

Some minor actions are "free" and don't inflict multi-action penalties. Speaking a short sentence or two, moving up to the character's Pace, falling prone, resisting opposed rolls, or dropping an item, are all examples of free actions.

One Wild Die Per Action

When Wild Cards roll multiple dice for a single action, such as when firing a machine gun, they roll only one Wild Die. A warrior with the Frenzy Edge, for example, rolls two Fighting dice and one Wild Die. He can use the Wild Die's total to replace either of his Fighting dice if he chooses. The Wild Die must either replace one of the regular dice or be ignored—it never adds another action or attack to the roll.

> *Example: Buck Savage captures a Tommy Gun from an evil cultist and turns it on the rest of the vile cabal. His Shooting is d12 and the weapon has a rate of fire of 3. He gets three d12s for the weapon's high rate of fire plus his Wild Die. Even if all the dice indicate success, he still only gets 3 hits—the Wild Die doesn't add an extra attack.*

Movement

Most humans can move their Pace (usually 6") in a round. This is considered a "free action." Other types of movement are covered below:

Crawling: A character may crawl 2" per turn. This counts as being prone when being fired upon.

Crouching: A character may move while crouching at half Pace. He may run while crouched (halve his total Pace after rolling for running). Ranged attacks against him suffer a –1 penalty.

Going Prone: A figure may fall prone at any time during its action. This usually counts as Medium Cover as well (see **Cover**).

Getting up costs 2" of movement. Smart characters in settings where lead is flying move, shoot, and then get prone behind cover before their action is over, forcing attackers to go on Hold to attack them.

Difficult Ground: Difficult ground such as mud, steep hills, or snow, slows characters down. Count each inch of difficult ground as two inches for purposes of movement.

Jumping: A character can jump 1" horizontally from a dead stop, or up to 2" with a "run and go." A successful Strength roll grants one extra inch of distance.

Running

A character may run an additional 1d6" during his turn if he wishes. Characters suffer a –2 penalty (the standard multi-action penalty) to all other actions made while running.

Group Running Rolls: When rolling for a group of nonplayer characters, villains, or monsters, the GM or controlling player makes a single running roll. The whole group doesn't actually *have to* run—it's just a convenient way to save a little time in the heat of battle.

Combat Actions

Characters can perform a multitude of actions when their card comes up in combat. The most common actions are making tests of wills, using a power, or attacking with the Fighting or Shooting skill. These are all covered on the following pages.

Simpler actions such as readying an item, drawing a sword, or other quick tasks usually take one action. More complex actions, such as lighting a torch, digging through a backpack to find a small item, and so on, might require a random number of rounds—say 1d6 rounds. The Game Master has the final say.

Readying Weapons

Drawing a weapon usually takes an entire round, but a character can do it faster if she wants. This is an action, however, and so inflicts the standard multi-action penalty of −2 the character's attack roll.

Drawing two weapons at once, drawing a weapon from a difficult location (such as an ankle holster or inside a coat), or drawing a large or unwieldy weapon (a rifle, a shotgun, etc.), follows the same procedure as outlined above but requires an Agility roll.

> *Example: Buck draws his machete and hacks at the spear-wielding cultists surrounding him. Buck doesn't want to take a full round to draw his weapon, so he takes the −2 penalty to his Fighting roll instead.*
>
> *If Buck wanted to draw his machete and his pistol, he could do so, but he'd have to make an Agility roll first. If he managed to do so, he'd suffer a −4 penalty to both his Fighting and Shooting (−2 for drawing and attacking, and another −2 for the additional attack).*

Attacks

The heart of *Savage Worlds* is its fast, furious combat. Here's everything you need to know to decimate your foes and keep your hero alive.

Fighting

A character may make one hand attack per round. The Target Number to hit is equal to the opponent's Parry score (2 plus half his Fighting ability; that's a 2 if he has no Fighting skill!).

Bonus Damage: If your attack hits with a raise, add +1d6 to your damage total as well! The d6 may Ace just like any other damage roll.

> *Example: Buck slices at a croc with his machete and hits with a raise. He makes a Strength roll and adds +d6 for the machete. Then he adds +1d6 to the total for his raise.*

Shooting & Throwing

The Shooting skill covers everything from pistols to rocket launchers. The base TN to hit something at Short range is 4 as usual. Shots at Medium range subtract 2 from the Shooting roll, and shots at Long range subtract 4 from the roll.

Bonus Damage: If you hit your target with a raise, add +1d6 to the damage total. This roll may Ace just like any other damage roll.

Range Modifiers

Range	Modifier
Short	—
Medium	–2
Long	–4

Rate of Fire

The Rate of Fire is how many Shooting dice the character rolls when firing the weapon. Many submachine guns, for example, have a Rate of Fire of 3, and therefore let the player roll up to 3 Shooting dice at once, at up to 3 different targets. These shots can be split among all possible targets as the player desires, but must all be taken at the same time. A shooter with an Uzi can't fire one shot, then move and fire two more, for instance.

Wild Cards roll one Wild Die as usual with the Shooting roll, and can use it in place of one of the Shooting dice if they choose.

Real automatic weapons can fire hundreds and even thousands of rounds per minute. We don't want to roll that many dice, track how many rounds are "lost" between targets, and so on, so each Shooting die actually represents several actual bullets. Each die rolled for a fully-automatic weapon represents a number of actual bullets equal to its rate of fire. An Uzi with a Rate of Fire of 3, for example, uses 3 rounds of ammunition per shot (or 9 bullets if it fires with all 3 dice). Don't worry about these "lost" bullets—they're already accounted for in the way autofire works in the game.

Most automatic weapons can be set to fire full-auto or single shot. Unless a weapon says otherwise, you can fire a single shot (and thereby ignore the automatic fire penalty of –2—see **Automatic Fire** on the next page).

Automatic weapons may also use the suppressive fire maneuver.

Example: Buck fires off his trusty Tommy Gun with a rate of fire of 3. That gives him 3 dice plus his Wild Die, though he can still only nominate and hit three possible targets. Firing all three possible shots uses up 9 actual rounds of ammunition.

SPECIAL RULES

Below are a number of rules for special maneuvers characters might perform during furious combat.

AIM

A character who spends a full round aiming (no movement allowed) may add +2 to his Shooting or Throwing roll in the following round versus whatever he aimed at (a person, vehicle, etc). Aiming for multiple rounds has no extra effect.

AREA EFFECT ATTACKS

Grenades, spell effects, and other attacks that cover a large area are "area effect attacks." The three most common size attacks have been made into Small, Medium, and Large Burst Templates, found on our website at www.peginc.com.

To attack with an area effect weapon, the character places the template on the table (or picks where he wants the center of the blast to be) and makes a Shooting or Throwing roll as usual. If the attack is successful, the blast is centered where desired. Everything under (or partially under) the template is affected. Roll damage separately for each target affected.

Failure means the blast deviates. Just how far depends on whether it was thrown or launched, and what range bracket the target was in (Short, Medium, or Long). Roll 1d6" for thrown weapons (such as grenades) and 1d10" for fired projectiles. Multiply by 1 for Short range, 2 for Medium, and 3 for Long.

Next roll a d12 and read it like a clock facing to determine the direction the missile deviates. A weapon can never deviate more than half the distance to the original target. That keeps things from going behind the thrower.

Unlike other attacks, raises on the attack roll do not add to damage to area effect attacks.

Cover: Targets who are prone or behind cover still get some protection from area-effect attacks. In these cases, the modifier they would normally receive against ranged attacks acts as that many points of Armor instead. A character in major cover, like a foxhole, negates four points of damage from a blast if he's caught within it.

Diving for Cover: Thrown weapons with a blast effect (such as grenades) and most artillery allow potential targets a chance to move out of the area of effect. Give targets who saw the danger coming an Agility roll at –2 to jump out of the way and avoid the damage. If successful, move the character just outside the template (his choice exactly where). Grenades can be thrown back as well (see below).

AUTOMATIC FIRE

Fully automatic fire (anything with a Rate of Fire of two or more) is less accurate than usual. The firer subtracts 2 from his Shooting rolls when firing such a weapon. Each die rolled on full-auto represents a number of bullets equal to the weapon's Rate of Fire.

BREAKING THINGS

Occasionally a character may want to break something, such as a weapon, a lock, or a door. Use the Toughness values below for these kinds of objects. Use these rules for solid objects. Larger objects with many components (such as vehicles) take multiple hits as per the vehicle rules.

Most anything can be broken given enough time and effort, so use this system only when attempting to break things in a hurry (such as during combat rounds).

The Parry of an inanimate object is 2. The catch is that damage rolls against them don't count bonuses from raises on the attack roll, nor Aces (even on Strength rolls in melee). Unlike a person or even a vehicle, an attack cannot hit a "vital" area on a lock or a door and thus do more damage. If an attack can't do enough damage to destroy an object, it can't destroy it (at least not quickly). This keeps characters from shattering swords with a feather and a lucky Strength roll.

Object Toughness

Object	Toughness	Damage Type
Light Door	8	Blunt, Cutting
Heavy Door	10	Blunt, Cutting
Lock	8	Blunt, Piercing
Handcuffs	12	Blunt, Piercing, Cutting
Knife, Sword	10	Blunt, Cutting
Rope	4	Cutting, Piercing
Small Shield	8	Blunt, Cutting
Medium Shield	10	Blunt, Cutting
Large Shield	12	Blunt, Cutting

If the damage roll equals or exceeds the object's Toughness, it's broken, bent, shattered, or otherwise ruined. The GM decides the exact effects—such as whether a good strike opens a hole in a door or knocks it off its hinges.

See **Obstacles** to attack *through* objects.

Damage Types: After the type of Object and its Toughness is the type of damage that can affect the object. Swords do cutting or piercing damage, spears are piercing weapons, and so on. Bullets are considered piercing weapons, though shotguns do blunt damage at close range for the purpose of this table.

The type of damage is important for objects because shooting a single bullet through a door, for instance, may penetrate it, but won't destroy it. Only a blunt or cutting attack is likely to destroy a door in one shot.

Called Shots

Use the following modifiers and effects when characters wish to target specific locations:

Limb (–2): An attack to a limb causes no additional damage but may ignore armor or have some other special effect (see the **Disarm** maneuver).

Head or Vitals (–4): The attacker gains +4 damage from a successful attack to these critical areas. The target must actually have vital areas, and the attacker must know where they are to gain this advantage.

Small Target (–4): Attacks against small targets such as the heart of a vampire or a missing scale on a large dragon's chest are made at –4. The effect of success depends on the situation–the vampire might die instantly, the missing scale may mean the dragon gets no armor, etc. If the GM has no particular effect in mind, it adds +4 damage just like a shot to the head or vitals.

Tiny Target (–6): Particularly small or narrow targets, such as the eye-slit of a knight's helmet, carry a –6 modifier. The effects of a hit depend on the target. In the case of the knight, the blow ignores armor and inflicts +4 damage because it's a head shot (as above).

Cover

Light Cover: Characters subtract 1 from their attack rolls if half or less of their target is obscured.

Medium Cover: The penalty is increased to –2 if more than half of the target is hidden from view. This is the usual penalty for attacking a prone character (see **Prone**).

Heavy Cover: The penalty is –4 if only a small part of the target is visible (prone beside a tree, behind a high wall, peeking around the corner of a building, etc).

Attacking through a very tight opening that provides near total cover, such as an arrow slit, subtracts 6 from enemy attack rolls.

Darkness

Darkness has a great effect on what can see and be seen.

Dim: Twilight, light fog, night with a full moon, and so on subtract 1 from combatants' attack rolls.

Dark: Normal darkness with some ambient light (starlight, partial moon) inflicts a –2 penalty, and targets aren't visible outside of 10".

Pitch Darkness: Targets aren't visible at all in pitch blackness, but if a character knows roughly where a victim is (he can hear him, target is in a confined space, a glint of light shines off his blade, etc.), he may be attacked at –4.

Defend

If a character's only regular action is to defend, his Parry is increased by +2 until his next action. The defender may move normally while performing this maneuver, but no running or other actions are allowed.

Disarm

A character can try to make an opponent drop a weapon (or other object) with either a close combat or a ranged attack. To cause a disarm check, the attacker must first hit the opponent's arm (–2, see **Called Shots**). The defender must then make a Strength roll. If the roll is less than the damage, he drops his weapon.

The attacker may choose to make this a nonlethal attack with a melee weapon. Ranged attacks can be nonlethal if the attacker targets the weapon instead of the limb (generally –4 instead of –2).

Double Taps & Three Round Bursts

A character with a semi-automatic weapon (such as a Colt .45, an M1 Carbine, or even an M16) can fire two shots in one action by "double-tapping." Double tapping is a single Shooting roll that gives the user +1 to hit

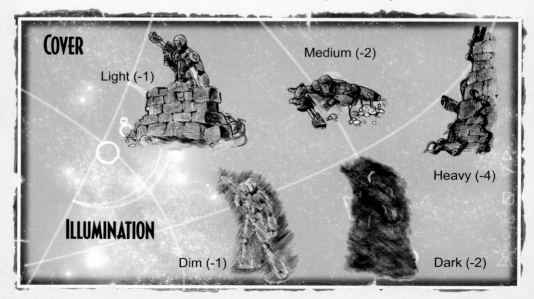

COVER

Light (-1)

Medium (-2)

Heavy (-4)

ILLUMINATION

Dim (-1)

Dark (-2)

and damage but expends two rounds of ammunition.

Many modern automatic weapons, such as the M16A2, have a selector switch that allows the user to go from single shot, to burst fire, to fully-automatic as a free action. Burst fire, or three-round bursts, gives the user +2 to hit and damage, and uses exactly three rounds of ammunition.

THE DROP

Sometimes an attacker is able to catch a foe off-guard and gets "the drop" on him. This usually happens at a distance of only a few feet, but other situations may occur (a sniper on a nearby rooftop).

Only the GM can determine when one character has obtained this kind of advantage over another. Usually it's when the victim is in the classic hostage pose, is completely unaware of the danger, or has been caught unarmed by an armed foe.

The attacker is considered on Hold and adds +4 to his attack and damage rolls should he decide to strike.

FINISHING MOVE

A completely helpless victim (bound, unconscious, etc) may be dispatched with a lethal weapon of some sort as an action. This is automatic unless the GM decides there's a special situation, such as a particularly tough or naturally armored victim, a chance for escape, and so on.

The killer must usually dispatch his foe up close and personal, but the GM may occasionally let finishing moves be performed at range.

FIRING INTO MELEE

Occasionally heroes have to fire into the middle of hand-to-hand fights. The trouble is that even though we might see figures standing perfectly still on the battle mat, in "reality," they're circling each other, wrestling back and forth, and moving erratically.

For that reason, firing into a tangle of people, such as a melee, is quite dangerous. Use the **Innocent Bystander** rules when this occurs (see below).

FULL DEFENSE

In addition to the usual Defend option, a character can go for a full defensive action. He makes a Fighting roll and uses the result as his Parry until his next action. This is a trait test, so he gets to roll his Wild Die as well. And, of course, the dice can Ace, and you can choose to use bennies on the roll if you want to.

Note that the character's Parry never gets worse as a result of the roll. If the roll is lower than the hero's Parry score, he keeps that instead (but gains no bonus from the full defense).

A hero using the full defense maneuver cannot move at all, however. He's doing everything he can to fend off whatever is attacking him. If you want to move away as well, use the Defend maneuver instead.

GANGING UP

Ganging up on a foe allows attackers to flank, exploit openings, and generally harass their outnumbered opponent.

Each additional adjacent foe adds +1 to all the attackers' Fighting rolls, up to a maximum of +4. If three warriors attack a single hero, for example, each of the three warriors gets a +2 bonus to their Fighting rolls.

GRAPPLING

Sometimes it's best to restrain an opponent rather than beat him to a bloody pulp. That's where grappling comes in.

Grappling is a regular Fighting roll, and is a non-damaging attack. If the attacker wins, he's entangled his foe. With a raise, his foe is also Shaken.

Once entangled, the defender may attempt to break free on his next action. Both the defender and attacker pick either their Strength or Agility and then an opposed roll is made. If successful, the defender is free but the attempt consumes his action. If he does so with a raise, he's free and may act normally. Failure means he is still entangled. Instead of breaking free the defender may attempt a different action but at a –4 penalty.

After grappling, the attacker may attempt to damage his victim on subsequent rounds by making an opposed roll as above. On a success he does his Strength in damage (gaining the extra d6 for a raise as normal).

INNOCENT BYSTANDERS

When an attacker misses a Shooting or Throwing roll, it may sometimes be important to see if any other targets in the line of fire were hit. The GM should only use this rule when it's dramatically appropriate—not for every missed shot in a hail of gunfire.

Each miss that comes up a 1 on the Shooting die indicates a random adjacent character was hit. If the attacker was firing on full-auto or with a shotgun, a roll of 1 or 2 hits the bystander. Roll damage normally.

Horses and other animals are possible targets when firing on mounted characters as well.

It's sometimes easier to hit an adjacent victim than the original target using this quick system. That may not be entirely realistic, but it's fast and simple, it makes large groups of people vulnerable to missile fire, and best of all, increases the drama of firing at opponents locked in melee with the attacker's allies.

NONLETHAL DAMAGE

A character who wants to beat someone up without killing them can choose to do nonlethal damage. This requires the attacker use only his fists or a blunt weapon of some sort. Edged weapons may be used if they have a flat side, but this subtracts –1 from the attacker's Fighting rolls.

Incapacitated Extras are simply knocked out for 1d6 hours. If a Wild Card suffers enough damage to be Incapacitated by a nonlethal attack, he makes a Vigor roll as usual. Check the Incapacitation table for a raise or success. Failures have a specific entry for nonlethal damage.

Nonlethal wounds are otherwise treated exactly as lethal wounds. This means it's much easier to render an Extra unconscious than a Wild Card. This is intentional, and should work well for most genres where heroes can take multiple punches before going down for the count, but most "mooks" go out with one or two good punches.

Example: Virginia is whacked on the head by a cultist. The villain gets lucky and does 4 wounds to our heroine. Virginia rolls her Vigor and gets a failure. Because he was doing nonlethal damage, Virginia is simply knocked out for 1d6 hours and has a temporary injury.

OBSTACLES

Sometimes characters have sufficient power to attack their foes *through* obstacles. (See the **Breaking Things** section to actually destroy intervening obstacles.)

To attack a target through an object, first decide if the attack hits. If it misses, there's no additional effect other than a small hole in the intervening obstacle.

If the attack would have hit without the cover modifier, the round is on target but the obstacle acts as armor for the target

Obstacle Toughness

Armor	Obstacle
+1	Glass, leather
+2	Plate glass window, shield
+3	Modern interior wall, sheet metal, car door
+4	Oak door, thick sheet metal
+6	Cinder block wall
+8	Brick wall
+10	Stone wall, bulletproof glass

behind it. In the chart above are the Armor bonuses for some obstacles commonly used as cover. This is added directly to the target's Toughness, including any actual armor he's wearing in the affected location. Subtract the weapon's Armor Piercing value from the total protection offered—not from *both* the obstacle and armor actually worn by the target.

Example: Buck blasts a cultist hiding behind a stone wall (Armor +10) with a bazooka. The bazooka ignores 9 points of Armor, so the wall only provides 1 point of protection.

Prone

Smart heroes lie down when lead starts flying. This gives them Medium Cover against most attacks. Attackers to the defender's side or within 3" ignore the modifier since the target is just as exposed as if he were standing to these characters.

A prone defender who is attacked in melee may automatically rise to defend himself if he desires. If he chooses to remain prone (or can't rise for some reason), his Parry is reduced by 2, and he must subtract 2 from his Fighting rolls.

Ranged Weapons in Close Combat

No ranged weapon larger than a pistol may be fired at adjacent foes engage in melee. Larger weapons may be used as clubs, however. Pistols can be fired in close combat, but since the defender is actively fighting back, the TN for the Shooting roll is his Parry rather than the standard TN of 4.

That means it's harder to hit someone who's wrestling with your character in melee than someone a few feet further who isn't actively wrestling with your hero.

Suppressive Fire

Instead of attacking specific targets, characters with fully automatic weapons can "spray" an area with lead in hopes of killing or suppressing a larger number of victims.

To suppress an area, the attacker places the Medium Burst Template on the battlefield and makes a single Shooting roll (regardless of the weapon's rate of fire). Include the standard modifiers for range, the full-auto penalty, and any other miscellaneous factors, but ignore the target's modifiers if any (such as being prone or in cover—these come into play in another way as you'll see below). If the attack misses, the spray is off-target and has no effect.

If the attack is successful, all possible targets within the area make Spirit rolls, adding any cover modifiers they would normally have against ranged attacks to this roll. Those who fail are Shaken. Those who roll a 1 on their Spirit die (regardless of any Wild Dice) are actually hit by the attack and suffer damage normally.

Ammo: Suppressive fire uses five times the weapon's Rate of Fire in bullets. A weapon with a Rate of Fire of 3, for example, uses 15 bullets for suppressive fire.

Example: Buck and Virginia are escaping from ancient ruins in a stolen biplane. Suddenly, they're swarmed by an evil alligator shaman and his brainwashed minions. Virginia spins the plane's Maxim gun around and fires. She uses suppressive fire to slow them down.

She places a Medium Burst Template 16" away—that's Medium Range for the Maxim—and rolls her Shooting. She gets a 13, −2 for full-auto, −2 for an unstable platform (the plane), and −2 for Medium range, for a total of 7. Success! The tribesmen in the template must roll their Spirit or be Shaken. Those who make it charge on through, but those who roll a 1 are hit!

TOUCH ATTACK

A character who simply wants to touch a foe (usually to deliver a magical effect of some kind) may add +2 to his Fighting roll.

TRICKS

Heroes often attempt fancy maneuvers or clever tricks to distract their foes and set them up for deadly follow-up attacks. This might include throwing sand in an opponent's eyes, ducking between a tall foe's legs to stab him in the back, and so on. Tricks do not include weapon feints—those are already "assumed" in a character's Fighting and Parry scores.

To perform the trick, the player must first describe exactly what his character is doing. Next he makes an opposed Agility or Smarts roll against his foe. The GM must determine which is more appropriate based on the player's description of the maneuver.

If the character is successful, his opponent is distracted and suffers −2 to his Parry until his next action. With a raise, the foe is distracted and Shaken as well.

These penalties do not stack. Tricking a foe twice has no additional effect.

Example: Buck is backed into a corner by a very large and dangerous thug. Our hero pulls the oldest trick in the book. He says "Hi Virginia!" and pretends to smile at someone behind his less-than-brilliant foe. He and the thug both make Smarts rolls, and Buck wins with a raise. The thug swirls about, expecting an attack from behind, and is momentarily Shaken. The unfortunate goon also suffers −2 to his Parry until his next action, giving Buck time for a quick rabbit punch that just might put the big fellow down.

TWO WEAPONS

A character may attack with a weapon in each hand if he desires. This works just like any other multi-action, and inflicts a −2 penalty to each attack. (Note that the Two-Fisted Edge negates the multi-action penalty when attacking with two weapons.)

Unless your hero is Ambidextrous, subtract another 2 points from the off-handed attack.

Example: Buck is backed into a corner by a pack of ravenous hyenas. He has two machetes, but isn't Ambidextrous. The first roll suffers a −2 penalty (for using two weapons), and the second suffers a −4 penalty (two weapons plus the off-hand penalty). He makes his Fighting roll twice, and gets his Wild Die with each roll.

Wild Attack

Sometimes a desperate character may want to throw caution to the wind and attack with everything he's got. This is called a "wild attack," and can be devastating if used correctly. If used recklessly, it can quickly get even a veteran character slaughtered.

Performing a wild attack adds +2 to the character's Fighting attack and resulting damage roll, but his Parry is reduced by 2 until his next action.

Wild attacks can be used with multiple attacks, such as from the Frenzy or Sweep Edges, or with two weapons.

Withdrawing From Close Combat

Inevitably, your hero may decide discretion is the better part of valor. Whenever a character retreats from melee, all adjacent non-Shaken opponents get an immediate free attack (but only one—no Frenzy or other Edges apply unless they specifically say otherwise).

A character may take the Defend option (+2 Parry) while retreating from combat, but won't be able to perform other actions that round besides movement and will still suffer the free attack.

Example: Buck is attacked by three cultists in melee. He decides to run for it, giving each cultist a free Fighting roll against him. Buck wisely uses the Defend maneuver as well to increase his Parry by +2 until he can get away.

Unarmed Defender

If one character has a melee weapon and his foe doesn't, the opponent is considered unarmed and is very likely in a world of hurt. Since he can only dodge and evade rather than parry, any armed attacker trying to hit him may add +2 to his Fighting roll. Nearly all animals and monsters are considered armed due to natural weapons such as claws and teeth.

Unstable Platform

A character attempting to fire a ranged attack from the back of a horse or other mount, a moving vehicle, or other "unstable platform" suffers –2 to his Shooting roll.

TESTS OF WILL

Intimidate and Taunt allow a character to make a "test of wills" attack against an opponent. In combat situations or during competitive miniature battles, tests of will have objective effects, as seen below. More subjective effects are outlined for the Game Master in roleplaying situations.

TESTS IN COMBAT

To make a test of wills, the character makes an opposed roll against his chosen target. The defender uses Smarts to resist Taunt, and Spirit to resist Intimidate.

The Game Master should modify both character's rolls depending on the situation. Waving a gun in someone's face isn't polite, but it's definitely worth a +2 bonus to Intimidate, for example (unless the target has an even bigger gun!).

A success means the attacker gets a +2 bonus to his next action against the defender during this combat. A raise on the roll gives the attacker the bonus and makes the defender Shaken as well.

This can be a great setup for an attack, a trick, or even a second test of wills if the first one didn't get a Shaken result.

"Attack" Skill		Resisted By...
Taunt	vs.	Smarts
Intimidate	vs.	Spirit

Example: Buck Savage tries to Taunt a crocodile cultist by flipping his machete and grinning like a hyena. He rolls his Taunt and beats the warrior's Smarts with a raise. The cultist is Shaken and Buck adds +2 to his next action against the spearman.

TESTS OUT OF COMBAT

Successfully Taunting or Intimidating a character has more subjective effects out of combat. An Intimidated foe might back down, retreat, or spill his guts about something the heroes want to know. An opponent who was humiliated with a really good Taunt might run away in shame—or he might be so infuriated he charges toward the hero and concentrates his attacks only on whoever made fun of him! This can be a really great way to distract a dangerous foe from a weaker ally.

Whatever the outcome, an attempted Taunt or Intimidate shifts the target's attitude one step towards Hostile (see **Reactions**).

TESTS OF WILL & GROUPS

A character can only make a test of wills attack against a single opponent. If the foe is the "leader" of a group, however, the rest of the crew is likely to follow his lead. If the boss of a group of bandits is Intimidated and decides to back down, for example, his minions follow his orders.

This is entirely subjective and depends on the situation, so the Game Master must make the call.

DAMAGE

After a successful close combat or ranged hit, the attacker rolls damage.

Ranged weapons do fixed damage, as listed in the Gear section.

Hand weapons do damage equal to the attacker's Strength die plus a second die, which depends on the weapon (a long sword, for instance, is a d8) and whether the wielder meets the minimum Strength requirement. An unarmed combatant rolls only his Strength die.

Wild Cards don't get their Wild Dice with any damage roll. All damage rolls can Ace, but you can't spend bennies on them.

BONUS DAMAGE

Well-placed attacks are more likely to hit vital areas, and so do more damage. If your hero gets a raise on his attack roll (regardless of how *many* raises), he adds +1d6 to the final total. This roll may Ace as usual!

DAMAGE EFFECTS

After hitting, damage is compared to the opponent's Toughness. If the damage roll is less than the target's Toughness, the victim is beaten up a bit but there's no game effect.

With a success, the victim is **Shaken**. If the victim is already Shaken, he suffers a **Wound** instead. Mark it with a counter of some sort to show its Shaken status (red gaming stones are perfect for this).

With a raise or better, Extras suffer a Wound, and wounded Extras are Incapacitated—they're injured badly enough to quit the fight, and may even be dead (see **Aftermath,** to find out for sure). Wounded Wild Cards are discussed below.

SHAKEN

Shaken characters are rattled, distracted, or momentarily shocked by tests of will results, fear, and most commonly, damage.

Being Shaken has several negative effects. First, Shaken characters may only move up to half their Pace and can perform no other actions (including running).

If a Shaken character is Shaken again by a damaging attack (not by a Test of Wills, fear, suppression, or similar non-damaging effect), he suffers a wound instead.

When it is his turn to act, a Shaken character first attempts to recover by making a Spirit roll. Failure means he remains Shaken. With a success, the recovery check consumes the hero's entire round but the character recovers and can remove his Shaken counter. With a raise, the character recovers instantly and may act normally. A player may also spend a benny immediately after attempting this roll to recover completely and still act normally this round.

Example: Virginia flaunts a little cleavage at a charging tribesman (she Taunts him and gets a Shaken result). Buck takes advantage of the distraction to slip in and knock the man silly with the flat of his machete. He does just enough damage to get a Shaken result. Since the warrior was already Shaken, he suffers a wound and goes down in a heap. The reverse would not have caused a wound. If Buck hits the tribesman first, Virginia's Shaken cannot wound him since it came from a Taunt.

WOUNDS AND WILD CARDS

Each raise on a damage roll over a Wild Card's Toughness causes a wound. Wild Cards can take three wounds before they are Incapacitated. (The "fourth" wound causes Incapacitation.)

Each wound a Wild Card suffers causes a −1 cumulative penalty to his Pace (minimum of 1) and to all further Trait tests-up to the maximum of a hero's 3 wounds. A hero with 2 wounds, for example, suffers a −2 penalty to his Pace and any Trait tests.

If a character suffers a wound and wasn't Shaken already, he's Shaken as well.

If a character is already Shaken, he suffers a wound as usual, but this isn't cumulative. Wild Cards only suffer one wound per raise whether they are Shaken or not.

INCAPACITATION

An Incapacitated hero must make an immediate Vigor roll, applying wound modifiers as applicable. This does not count as an action.

Raise: The hero is only stunned. The hero still has 3 wounds, but is not Incapacitated. He is Shaken and suffers a temporary impairment as well. Roll 2d6 on the Injury Table. The effects are short-term and go away when the combat is over.

Success: The hero is unconscious. He regains consciousness with a successful Healing roll, as noted above, or after an hour has passed. Roll 2d6 on the Injury Table. The injury goes away when all wounds are healed.

Failure: The victim is Bleeding Out. At the start of each round, he must make another Vigor roll (with applicable penalties). A failure means he has to roll again next round. A result of 1 or less means the poor sap dies (as a Critical Failure).

Success means he stabilizes but remains unconscious until healed. Roll 2d6 on the Injury Table as well. The injury is permanent and requires specialist healing (such as the greater healing power).

With nonlethal damage, treat this as a Success except the hero is unconscious for 1d6 hours.

Critical Failure: The hero is dead. Nothing can bring him back. With nonlethal damage, treat this as a Success except the hero is unconscious for 2d6 hours.

Injury Table

Roll 2d6 on the table below. If the attack that caused the Injury was directed at a specific body part, use that location instead of rolling randomly.

2d6	Wound
2	**Unmentionables:** If the injury is permanent, reproduction is out of the question without miracle surgery or magic.
3-4	**Arm:** Roll the left or right arm randomly; it's rendered useless.
5-9	**Guts:** Your hero catches one somewhere between the crotch and the chin. Roll 1d6:

  1-2 Broken: Agility reduced a die type (min d4).

  3-4 Battered: Vigor reduced a die type (min d4).

  5-6 Busted: Strength reduced a die type (min d4).

| 10 | **Leg:** Roll left or right leg randomly. It's rendered uselss and Pace reduced –1. |
| 11-12 | **Head:** A grievous injury to the head. Roll 1d6:: |

  1-2 Hideous Scar: Your hero now has the Ugly Hindrance.

  3-4 Blinded: An eye is damaged. Gain the One Eye Hindrance (or the Blind Hindrance if he only had one good eye).

  5-6 Brain Damage: Massive trauma to the head. Smarts reduced one die type (min d4).

Example: Buck has been Shaken by a Taunt when a frenzied croc makes two successful attacks. The first one just beats his Toughness, and since Buck is already Shaken, he takes a wound. The second attack gets two raises! Buck takes two wounds (it doesn't matter that he was already Shaken).

Incapacitation

A Wild Card is Incapacitated when he takes more than three wounds (after **Soaking**). He is out of the fight until he receives healing. Exactly how many wounds the hero takes is irrelevant—anything over 3 wounds means Incapacitation.

Incapacitated characters are too beaten, battered, or bruised, to do anything useful. They may not perform actions and are not dealt action cards in combat. See the **Incapacitated Heroes** chart on the previous page for what happens next.

Timing

Characters sometimes take multiple hits on the same action card, such as when they're ganged up on by a group of bad guys. The game has been designed to let players roll all the attack dice at once to keep things fast and furious. Damage rolls, however, are resolved and applied one at a time. The attacker can decide what order to roll his damage in if it becomes an issue. This is especially useful when you're doing large skirmishes and rolling lots of dice together.

Multiple Incapacitated Results

A hero can suffer multiple Incapacitated results at the same time. If he is Incapacitated and takes another wound, he must make another Vigor roll.

The character suffers any additional injuries from rolling on the Injury Table, but his condition can never improve, only stay the same or worse.

The Soak Roll

A character can spend a benny to automatically eliminate a Shaken condition (see **Shaken,** below).

If the benny is spent immediately after taking one or more wounds from a single attack, you may make a Vigor roll as well. A success and each raise on the roll reduces the number of wounds suffered from that attack by 1. If the character is left with *any* wounds from the attack however, he's still Shaken as usual. Don't count the wound modifiers you're *about* to suffer when making this roll.

A character may only make one soak roll per attack. If a soak roll eliminates 2 of 3 wounds, for instance, a hero can't make another soak roll to eliminate the third wound. (The hero *could* spend a second benny to reroll the Vigor roll as usual, however.)

If a character suffers multiple hits on the same action card, he needs to spend bennies and make soak rolls after each result—before the next "set" of wounds is soaked.

Example: Buck gets attacked and hit twice in the same round by two crocodile cultists. The first attack makes him Shaken, and the second causes 2 wounds.

Buck takes the first result and is Shaken. He knows if he completely soaks the second, he won't be Shaken anyway. Now he makes a Soak roll against the two wounds and gets a 5 on his Vigor roll. That negates one wound, but he remains Shaken. He could now spend another benny to be unshaken, but can't negate the remaining wound.

HEALING

The Healing skill can be used to treat wounded characters after a battle. (Only magical healing works fast enough to be used during a battle.)

Each attempt takes 10 minutes, and requires some basic supplies such as bandages and reasonably clean water. If these aren't available, the healer suffers a −2 penalty to his roll. The healer must also subtract the patient's wound levels from his skill roll.

Note as well that a wounded healer subtracts any penalties for his own wounds from the roll as well. A wounded character trying to heal his own injuries suffers double the wound penalty—once for the actual pain caused by his wounds, and once for their actual severity.

A success removes one wound, and a raise removes two. Medics can reattempt their healing roll as often as they like within one hour of the wound being received—after this, only natural healing or the *greater healing* spell can help.

A result of 1 or less, however, means the patient suffers an additional wound. A hero who is already Incapacitated must make another Vigor roll. The Incapacitation must be treated before any wounds may be tended, which takes valuable time.

A character who became Incapacitated due to wounds becomes Shaken if Healed (whether natural magical) but still has 3 wounds. A second Healing roll may be attempted to tend to any actual wounds suffered. Heroes Incapacitated by Fatigue must be treated for the specific cause of their stress in order to recover.

AFTERMATH

After a battle, the players make Vigor rolls for all of their wounded allies (the GM may roll for wounded foes). With a success, that character is alive but Incapacitated (failure indicates death). With a raise, the wounds were only superficial and the character may function normally. This creates interesting choices for the players after battle as they must decide what to do with their wounded companions and living captives.

Walking Wounded: If it becomes important to know which Incapacitated characters can walk and which cannot, make a second Vigor roll for each. Those who make it are "walking wounded"—they may shamble slowly but still cannot fight or perform other useful actions.

Those who don't make the roll can be moved but risk aggravating their injuries. They must make another Vigor roll for each and every hour of movement. Should they fail, they begin to die. They may be stabilized with a Healing roll at −2, but any further movement will no doubt be fatal.

Natural Healing

Every five days, wounded or Incapacitated characters may make Vigor rolls. Wild Cards remove one wound level (or their Incapacitated status) with a success, or improve two steps with a raise. A critical failure on a natural healing roll increases a Wild Card's wound level by one. If the hero already has three wounds he becomes Incapacitated. Extras lose their Incapacitated status with a success and expire if they roll a 1 on their Vigor die.

Subtract wound penalties from these rolls as usual, as well as any of the modifiers below. These are cumulative, so rough traveling in intense cold with one wound is a total penalty of −5, for example.

Medical attention means that someone with the Healing skill is actively checking the patient's wounds, changing dressings, giving what medicines are available, and generally looking after the patient's well-being.

Natural Healing Modifiers

Modifier	Condition
−2	Rough traveling
−2	No medical attention
−2	Poor environmental conditions, such as intense cold, heat, or rain
—	Medical Attention (1940 or earlier)
+1	Medical Attention (1941 or better)
+2	Medical Attention (2010 and beyond)

Attack Options Summary

Attack	Penalty
Aim	+2 Shooting/Throwing if character does not move
Area Effect Attacks	Targets under template suffer damage, treat cover as armor; missed attack rolls cause 1d6" deviation for thrown weapons, 1d10" for launched weapons; x1 for Short, x2 for Medium, x3 for Long
Autofire	See rules
Breaking Things	See Obstacle Toughness Table; Parry 2; No bonus damage or Aces
Called Shots	Limb –2; Head –4, +4 damage, Small target –4; Tiny target –6
Cover	Light –1; Medium –2; Heavy –4
Darkness	Dim –1; Dark –2, targets are not visible beyond 10"
Pitch Darkness	Targets must be detected to be attacked at –4
Defend	+2 Parry; character may take no other actions
Disarm	–2 attack; defender makes Str roll vs. damage or drops weapon
Double Tap/ 3 Rd Burst	+1 attack and damage/+2 attack and damage
The Drop	+4 attack and damage
Finishing Move	Instant kill to helpless foe with lethal weapon
Firing Into Melee	See Innocent Bystanders
Full Defense	Fighting roll replaces Parry if higher
Ganging Up	+1 Fighting per additional attacker; maximum of +4
Grappling	Fighting roll to grapple. Raise=opponent Shaken; Defender makes opposed Strength or Agility to break free (any other action made at –4); Attacker can make opposed Str or Agility to cause damage
Innocent Bystanders	Missed Shooting or Throwing roll of 1 (2 with shotguns or autofire) hits random adjacent target
Nonlethal Damage	Characters are knocked out instead of potentially killed when Incapacitated
Obstacles	If attack hits by the concealment penalty, the obstacle acts as Armor
Prone	As Medium cover; prone defenders are –2 Fighting, –2 Parry
Ranged Weapons in Close Combat	Pistols only; Target Number is defender's Parry
Suppressive Fire	With successful Shooting roll, targets in Med Burst Template make a Spirit roll or be Shaken; roll of1 are hit for normal damage
Touch Attack	+2 Fighting
Trick	Describe action; make opposed Agility or Smarts roll; opponent is –2 Parry until next action; with a raise, foe is –2 Parry and Shaken
Two Weapons	–2 attack; additional –2 for off-hand if not Ambidextrous
Unarmed Defender	Armed attackers gain +2 Fighting
Unstable Platform	–2 Shooting from a moving vehicle or animal
Wild Attack	+2 Fighting; +2 damage; –2 Parry until next action
Withdrawing from Close Combat	Adjacent foes get one free attack at retreating character

Chapter Four:
Arcane Backgrounds

Most roleplaying games feature "magic" in one form or another. Whether it's hidden occult lore practiced only by dark cultists, voodoo rituals, the eldritch sorcery of powerful wizards, weird gadgets created by mad scientists, superpowers, or the psionic powers of the mind, these rules handle it all in one simple system.

For ease of use, we call all of these effects "powers." Best of all, powers work the same from game to game, but the particular use and trappings give the same powers endless variations. That means you can create wizards, mad scientists, superheroes, and even creatures with one simple set of easy-to-remember rules.

Making Arcane Characters

Before we go any further, you need to make sure your GM will allow arcane characters in his game. You can't make a wizard in a realistic military campaign, and mad scientists might not fit in every fantasy setting.

Now that that's out of the way, you need to buy the Arcane Background Edge and choose which type of supernatural power your hero is blessed with.

Five different types of powers are presented in this rulebook: Magic, Miracles, Psionics, Super Powers, and Weird Science. All types of powers use the same basic mechanics but with a few important differences in the details.

Let's talk about what's similar before we get into what's different.

Arcane Skill

Each type of power has a particular arcane skill: Faith for miracles, Psionics for psionics, Spellcasting for magic, and Weird Science for weird science. Super powers use skills a little differently, as you'll see on the following pages.

You need to take the skill for your character's particular Arcane Background and put points into it as usual. You'll find the attribute the skill is linked to in parentheses beside the skill itself.

Power Points

Arcane characters energize their powers with "Power Points." As soon as you buy an Arcane Background Edge, your hero gets the listed number of Power Points.

Using a power requires that you spend a number of these points. Some powers allow you to pay additional points for better effects, and some allow you to maintain the effect by spending Power Points each round.

Heroes recover 1 Power Point per hour.

Starting Powers

Arcane characters start with a number of powers dictated by their particular Arcane Background. See the Arcane Background list for specifics.

Learning New Powers

An arcane character can learn a new power by selecting the New Power Edge. As soon as he levels up and chooses this Edge, he can instantly begin using whichever power he chooses.

Using Powers

As an action, a character may use a single power by declaring the power he's using, spending the desired number of Power Points, and making an arcane skill roll.

If the roll is failed, there's no effect but the Power Points are lost. If successful, consult the particular power to determine the results.

Some powers have variable effects depending on how many Power Points are used to cast them. The player must spend the desired Power Points *before* rolling his character's arcane skill to see if he's successful.

Maintaining Powers

Some powers may be maintained, as listed in the power's Duration description. This is a free action. The number following the duration is the cost in Power Points to keep the power going. No new skill roll is needed to maintain a power.

For each power currently being maintained, the caster suffers a −1 to future arcane skill rolls (but not other Trait tests). A wizard maintaining *armor* and *charm*, for example, suffers a −2 penalty to his Spellcasting rolls until he allows those powers to lapse. He does *not* suffer penalties to his Fighting (or other) rolls while these spells are being maintained.

Disruption

A character who is actively maintaining a power may be disrupted if he suffers damage. To maintain concentration for *all* of his powers, the hero makes one opposed arcane skill roll versus the damage he suffered. If his roll is higher, he maintains all of his spells. If he fails, he instantly drops all of his powers *after* the attack that caused the disruption is resolved.

A character who is Shaken by non-damaging means (such as a Test of Wills) must make a simple Smarts roll to maintain his powers.

Arcane Backgrounds

Below are the five different types of Arcane Backgrounds. Each type describes the Arcane Skill a character with that background uses, his starting Power Points, the number of powers he starts play with, and any potential drawbacks to the power (such as Backlash or Malfunctions).

Arcane Background (Magic)

Arcane Skill: Spellcasting (Smarts)
Starting Power Points: 10
Starting Powers: 3

Magicians range from powerful wizards to vile cultists. They draw on raw supernatural energy to fuel their eldritch fires. This energy often infuses the worlds in which they live, and is drawn forth with elaborate rituals, words of power, runes, or perhaps even dark sacrifices.

Wizards are often quite weak early in their careers, but are forces to be reckoned with as they become powerful sorcerers.

• **Backlash:** When a wizard rolls a 1 on his Spellcasting die (regardless of his Wild Die), he is automatically Shaken. This can cause a wound.

Arcane Background (Miracles)

Arcane Skill: Faith (Spirit)
Starting Power Points: 10
Starting Powers: 2

Those who draw on miracles are priestly types or holy champions. Their power comes from a divine presence of some sort, including gods, nature, or spirits. Their powers are usually invoked with a few words of prayer or by performing established rituals.

Protector: Those who cast miracles are champions of their particular religions. Good priests vow to protect the innocent, fight evil, and obey all other tenets of their particular religion. Evil priests typically vow to defeat those who oppose their religion, or simply to cause as much misery and strife as possible. The player and Game Master should come up with a simple list of what is important to the character's religion and use this as a guide.

Champions who violate their beliefs are temporarily or permanently forsaken by their chosen deity. Minor sins give the character a –2 to his Faith rolls for one week. Major sins rob him of all arcane powers for one week. Mortal sins cause the character to be forsaken until the penitent hero completes some great quest or task of atonement to regain his lost powers.

Arcane Background (Psionics)

Arcane Skill: Psionics (Smarts)
Starting Power Points: 10
Starting Powers: 3

Psionicists have discovered how to tap into their own psychic powers. They can manipulate matter, create fire, or control their own bodies with but a thought.

• **Brainburn:** When a psionic character rolls a 1 on his Psionics die (regardless of his Wild Die), he is automatically Shaken. On a critical failure, the character lets out a psychic scream that causes him to be Shaken along with all allies in a Large Burst Template who fail a Spirit roll. This can cause a wound.

Arcane Background (Super Powers)

Arcane Skill: Special (None)
Starting Power Points: 20
Starting Powers: 1

Characters with super powers gain their abilities through strange circumstances, such as being bitten by irradiated creatures, exposure to strange chemicals, or perhaps by finding alien artifacts. This particular level of power is intended for relatively low-level "pulp" heroes. More powerful super types are dealt with in specific Savage Settings.

Super powers work a little differently from most other Arcane Backgrounds—each power is its own skill and has no linked attribute. A hero with the *armor* and *bolt* powers, for example, also has an Armor and a Bolt skill he uses to enable it. That means it's more expensive for a character to improve his powers, but he starts with more Power Points than other arcane types so that he can use his abilities more often.

Best of all, there are no drawbacks for super powers as there are with other types of arcane powers—the power either works or it doesn't.

Arcane Background (Weird Science)

Arcane Skill: Weird Science (Smarts—see below)
Starting Power Points: 10 (but see below)
Starting Powers: 1

Weird Science is the creation of strange and powerful devices. It differs from regular science in that some element of the arcane is involved. Maybe it's just generic "super-science," or perhaps it's divinely (or demonically) inspired. Maybe the science itself is relatively sound, but it derives power from an arcane source, such as ghost rock in *Deadlands*, or some other magical mineral or essence in a steampunk fantasy game.

Weird Science is also different in that each new power is actually a new "gizmo." The player must write down exactly what the device is when he gains the power.

An inventor with the *invisibility* power, for instance, actually has an *invisibility* belt, cloak, etc. Players are encouraged to give their devices pseudo-scientific names as well ("Dr. Zee's chromatic disfibulating device!").

Each device comes with its own Power Points equal to the inventor's Power Points. An inventor with the *bolt* power and 10 Power Points, for example, could make a ray gun that fires electrical beams. The gun has 10 Power Points it can use to fire the beams just like a wizard would cast the *bolt* spell.

Malfunction: Weird science devices are never perfect technology. They often suffer from frequent, spectacular, and deadly malfunctions.

If a gadgeteer uses a device and rolls a 1 on his skill die (regardless of his Wild Die), it has malfunctioned in some way. The gadgeteer may not use that power again until it's repaired, which requires a Repair roll and 2d6 hours worth of work.

More on Weird Science

Weird Science is a little more complicated than other Arcane Backgrounds. If you just want to hurl a few fireballs, try out magic or psionics. If you're willing to go through a few more steps than usual, however, you'll find Weird Science powerful, flexible, and fun!

It's very important to understand that Weird Science isn't used to make mundane devices, even if they are extraordinary. As long as they're possible and aren't too far above the given tech level of the world, they're just "high-tech." Only actual weird science, inspired by, created by, or powered by some sort of supernatural force qualifies.

It's also important to remember that Weird Science doesn't allow a character to make anything he wants. He can only make a device that utilizes one of the powers in this book (or an appropriate Savage Setting).

Arcane Skill: Weird Science is the skill an inventor uses when activating his force-field belt (the *armor* or *deflection* power) or his hypno-ray (the *puppet* power).

If a device uses a different skill, such as Driving, Fighting, or Shooting, the inventor uses that instead. A ray gun, for example, uses the Shooting skill, while a "vibroknife" (a knife with the *smite* power) uses Fighting.

Using Gizmos: To activate a "passive" device (generally those powers which may be maintained) such as an *invisibility* belt, the character makes a Weird Science roll. Raises may increase the effects of the power as usual. It is then activated and may be used normally.

Powers that require an opposed roll, such as *puppet,* also use the scientist's Weird Science skill.

Active devices, such as ray guns, function as they are used. The inventor makes a Shooting or Fighting attack as appropriate and marks off the number of Power Points drained. Such rolls are still subject to Malfunction on a Fighting or Shooting roll of 1, however (as above).

New Powers: Each time a Weird Scientist takes the New Power Edge, he has invented a new gadget. He simply chooses a power and decides what kind of gizmo it's contained in as usual. He can also repeat a power he's already taken. A mad scientist might want to create two ray-guns, for example, so that he can use one and give one to a companion.

Maintaining Powers: Because weird scientists use inventions rather than cast spells, they don't suffer any penalties for maintaining powers, but their devices still pay the maintenance costs in Power Points as usual.

Sharing: An inventor can hand his device over to a companion to use. The device works the same for the companion as it does for the owner. If the Weird Science skill is required however, the companion will have to make a default roll as usual. That means gizmos are much more effective when used by weird scientists than in the hands of others.

Recharging: Devices regain Power Points just like a character, at the rate of 1 point per hour. Recharging may represent the device being plugged into an outlet, gathering solar rays, or simply getting new ammunition (whatever that might be). Regardless of the description, however, it regains Power Points at the rate of one per hour just like other power types.

The Power Edges Rapid Recharge and Improved Rapid Recharge apply to all of the inventor's devices rather than the inventor himself.

Soul Drain: Weird Scientists cannot take the Soul Drain Edge.

More Power Points: When an inventor gains more Power Points, he's assumed to tinker with his existing devices and upgrade them as well. This means *all* of his devices gain the additional Power Points. In effect, if an inventor has 20 Power Points, all of his devices have 20 Power Points as well.

Losing Devices: If an inventor's gizmo is taken away, lost, or destroyed, he can make another in 2d6 hours as long as he has access to a workshop and the proper components. This requires a Repair roll. A raise halves the time needed to create the device.

If the original should somehow be returned, it no longer functions (the character doesn't get a "free" duplicate in this way).

Example: Doctor Gold starts play with a vibroknife (the smite *power) and 10 Power Points. Later on, he levels up and chooses the New Power Edge. With that he invents a ray-gun with the* bolt *power. Both devices have 10 Power Points.*

In a fight, Doctor Gold first "turns on" his vibroknife by making a Weird Science roll. He gets a raise so the knife does +4 damage for its duration. The ray-gun doesn't have to be activated. The Doc simply makes a Shooting roll whenever he fires it (just like a mage would make a Spellcasting roll).

POWERS

Listed below are a number of powers available in most Savage Settings. Each power has the following statistics:

Rank: This is the Rank a character must be in order learn this power; Novice, Seasoned, Veteran, Heroic, or Legendary.

Power Points: The number of points it costs to use the power. Some powers allow the character to pay additional points for additional effects. This is always determined—and paid for—before the dice are rolled.

Range: The maximum distance the target of the power can be from the user when the power is first activated (it remains in effect even if the target moves out of range as long as it's maintained). A Range of Smarts, for example, means 10" for a character with a Smarts of d10. If a power lists three ranges, such as 12/24/48, these are read just like missile weapon ranges, and subtract the standard penalties for each range bracket (0/–2/–4). The arcane character's skill roll acts as both his "casting" and attack total for these type powers (Weird Scientists use Fighting or Shooting as usual instead).

Duration: How long the power lasts in rounds. A power with a Duration of 1 lasts until the heroes' next action. A duration of 2 means it lasts for two actions, and so on.

If the Duration of a power has a second entry in parentheses, such as 3 (1/round), it means the power has a duration of 3 rounds and may then be maintained from round to round by spending the listed number of Power Points (1 in this case). Each power maintained subtracts 1 from future uses of the hero's arcane skill.

Trappings: The powers listed in this chapter are designed to be as simple to use and remember as possible. This helps the Game Master remember what all the powers do, and helps players remember the rules for common powers even between different settings. But just because these powers work

the same from setting to setting doesn't mean they have to look the same or even have the same names (at least among the characters of the world). The *bolt* power, for example, is a very simple but flexible power. In your high-fantasy, game, it might be called "magic missile" and take the form of yellow bolts of light. In your dark magic and crazed cultists game, the same power could be the ranged attack of an insect shaman that takes the form of a swarm of killer bees that rushes toward the heroes and stings them!

When the GM decides to dramatically change the trappings of a power, she'll also have to figure out any special rules that go with them. If an *armor* spell forms a blazing shield of fire, for instance, perhaps it offers double protection against fire attacks, but none against bolts of cold or ice (or vice-versa). Similarly, if a power is tied to an item, such as a witch using a broom for the *fly* power, you'll need to decide what happens if the item is taken away. Check out the sidebar on the following page for a couple of examples.

or ice. (If you're using a gridded mat to play, draw the *barrier* between the squares directly along the grid-lines.) The exact placement of each section is defined by the caster, but each section must be connected to at least one other section after the first.

When the spell expires or a section is broken, it crumbles to dust or otherwise dissipates (the trappings are never left behind).

Each section of the barrier may be destroyed by an attack that exceeds its Toughness of 10. Hitting the wall is automatic with a Fighting attack (ranged attacks must roll to hit as usual), but raises on the attack roll do not grant bonus damage.

Opponents may climb the barrier at −2 to their Climb roll if it is made of something solid. Fiery versions of the *barrier* cause 2d4 damage to anyone who wishes to leap through instead.

ARMOR

Rank: Novice
Power Points: 2
Range: Touch
Duration: 3 (1/round)
Trappings: A mystical glow, hardened skin, ethereal armor, a mass of insects or worms, densening.

Armor creates a field of magical protection around a character, or an actual shell of some sort, effectively giving the target Armor. Success grants the recipient 2 points of Armor. A raise grants 4 points of Armor.

BARRIER

Rank: Seasoned
Power Points: 1/section
Range: Smarts
Duration: 3 (1 per section, per round)
Trappings: Fire, ice, thorns, force, bones.

Barrier creates a solid, immobile wall to protect the user against attack or to entrap an opponent.

Regardless of what the *barrier* is made of (ice, thorns, stone, energy, etc.), it has a Toughness of 10. Every Power Point spent creates a 1" wide section of wall. The *barrier* ranges in width from a few "real world" inches thick for stone or other hard materials up to a foot for things like bones

BEAST FRIEND

Rank: Novice
Power Points: Special
Range: Smarts x 100 yards
Duration: 10 minutes
Trappings: The mage concentrates and gestures with his hands.

This spell allows mages to speak with and guide the actions of nature's beasts. It works only on creatures with animal intelligence, not humanoids. Nor does it work on conjured, magical, or otherwise "unnatural" animals.

The target must be within the sorcerer's range—it is not conjured.

The cost to control a creature depends on its Size. The base cost is 3, plus twice its Size for creatures with a Size greater than 0. A great white shark (Size +4) costs 3 plus

(2x4=) 8 or 11 points. A roc (Size +8) costs 19 Power Points to control.

Swarms may also be controlled. Small swarms cost 3, Mediums 5, and Large 8. Thus a single rat costs 3 to control, as does a small swarm of the creatures.

BLAST

Rank: Seasoned
Power Points: 2-6
Range: 24/48/96
Duration: Instant
Trappings: Balls of fire, ice, light, darkness, colored bolts, swarm of insects.

Blast is an area effect power that can put down many opponents at once. The character first picks where he wants to center the *blast,* then makes the appropriate skill roll. Normal ranged attack modifiers apply.

The area of effect is a Medium Burst Template (found at our website). If the roll is failed, the *blast* deviates as a launched projectile.

Targets within the *blast* suffer 2d6 damage. Unlike other attacks, raises on the attack roll do not add to damage to area effect attacks.

Additional Effects: For double the Power Points, the blast does 3d6 damage *or* is the size is increased to a Large Burst Template. For triple the points, it does both.

BOLT

Rank: Novice
Power Points: 1-6
Range: 12/24/48
Duration: Instant
Trappings: Fire, ice, light, darkness, colored bolts, insects.

Bolt is a standard attack power of wizards, and can also be used for ray guns, bursts of energy, streaks of holy light, and other ranged attacks. The damage of the *bolt* is 2d6.

Additional Bolts: The character may cast up to 3 *bolts* by spending a like amount of Power Points. This must be decided before the power is cast. The *bolts* may be spread among targets as the character chooses.

MORE ON TRAPPINGS

Here are a couple of examples of how you can tailor powers for your setting. We don't recommend detailing every such power, but spicing up a few of the most common can really make each setting feel quite different.

SWARM OF BEES (BOLT)

When cast, a swarm of bees races from the cultist's hands and overwhelms a foe with hundreds of stings. The bees cannot penetrate thick material, however, so anyone in a completely sealed suit of some kind is immune to the effects.

FIRE SHIELD (ARMOR)

A blazing shield of fire erupts in front of the wizard for the duration of the spell. It protects only to the front, but causes 2d6 damage to anyone he successfully hits with it. It also offers double protection against fire-based attacks, but no protection against cold-based attacks.

BEDKNOBS AND BROOMSTICKS (FLY)

This spell allows a witch to fly, just like the power In this world, however, the witch must have a broomstick, a bed, or a small carpet. If no such component is available, the spell cannot be cast.

Firing the additional bolts does not incur any attack penalties.

Additional Damage: The character may also increase the damage to 3d6 by doubling the Power Point cost per *bolt*. This may be combined with the additional bolts, so firing 3 *bolts* of 3d6 damage costs 6 Power Points.

Boost/Lower Trait

Rank: Novice
Power Points: 2
Range: Smarts
Duration: 3 (1/Round)
Trappings: Physical change, glowing aura, potions.

This power allows a character to increase any of a target's Traits by one die type for a standard success, and two with a raise. The affected Trait can exceed d12. Each step over d12 adds +1 to his Trait total. For example, a raise on someone who already has a d12 in the affected Trait grants him d12+2 for the duration of the power.

The power can also be used to lower an opponent's Trait. This is an opposed roll against the victim's Spirit. Success lowers any Trait of the caster's choice one step, a raise lowers it two steps. A Trait cannot be lowered below a d4. Multiple castings stack, though the caster must keep track of when each casting expires as usual.

Burrow

Rank: Novice
Power Points: 3
Range: Smarts x 2
Duration: 3 (2/round)
Trappings: Dissolving into the earth and appearing elsewhere.

Burrow allows a mage standing on raw earth to meld into it. He can remain underground if he wants in a sort of "limbo" or *burrow* to anywhere within his range. A mage with a Smarts of d8 could therefore move up to 16" (32 yards) on the first round, maintain the spell and stay submerged for the second and "move" another 16".

A *burrowing* earth mage can attempt to surprise a foe (even one who saw him *burrow*) by making an opposed Stealth versus Notice roll. If the mage wins, he gains +2 to attack and damage that round, or +4 with a raise. Targets on Hold may attempt to interrupt the attack as usual.

Burst

Rank: Novice
Power Points: 2
Range: Flame Template
Duration: Instant
Trappings: A shower of flames, light, or other energy.

Burst produces a large fan of energy that bathes its targets in red-hot fire or other damaging energy.

When cast, place the thin end of the Cone Template at the character's front. Targets within the template may make Agility rolls versus the caster's arcane skill roll to avoid the blaze. Those who fail suffer 2d10 damage. This counts as a Heavy Weapon.

With a fire trapping, victims have a 1 in 6 chance of catching fire as well (see the **Fire** rules).

DEFLECTION

Rank: Novice
Power Points: 2
Range: Touch
Duration: 3 (1/round)
Trappings: Mystical shield, gust of wind, phantom servant that intercepts the missiles.

Deflection powers work in a variety of ways. Some actually deflect incoming attacks, others blur the target's form or produce other illusionary effects. The end result is always the same however—to misdirect incoming melee and missile attacks from the user.

With a standard success, attackers must subtract 2 from any Fighting, Shooting, or other attack rolls directed at the user. A raise increases the penalty to –4. This also acts as Armor against area effect weapons.

DETECT/CONCEAL ARCANA

Rank: Novice
Power Points: 2
Range: Sight
Duration: 3 (1/round) *or* 1 hour (1/hour)
Trappings: Waving hands, whispered words.

Detect/conceal arcana allows a character to sense supernatural persons, objects, or effects within sight. This includes invisible foes, enchantments on people or items, mad science devices, and so on.

The power can also be reversed to conceal a single supernatural item, being, or effect. This has the same cost, but the duration is much longer—1 hour with a maintenance cost of 1 per hour. When used in this way, those who wish to see through the ruse with *detect arcana* use their arcane skill roll as an opposed roll against the concealer's skill (rolled anew each time *detect arcana* is cast). The detecting character may only attempt to see through concealed powers once per fresh casting.

DISPEL

Rank: Seasoned
Power Points: 3
Range: Smarts
Duration: Instant
Trappings: Waving hands, whispered words.

Dispel allows a hero to negate enemy spells, miracles, mad science, or super powers. It has no effect on innate powers, such as a dragon's breath or a banshee's scream. Neither does *dispel* work on magic items or permanent enchantments unless the specific item or enchantment says otherwise.

Dispel can be used on a power already in effect, and can also be used to counter an enemy power as it's being used. The latter requires the countering mage to be on Hold and interrupt his foe's action as usual.

In either case, *dispelling* the opponent's power is an opposed roll of arcane skills. The *dispelling* character suffers a –2 modifier if the target power is of another type (magic vs. miracles, superpowers vs. mad science, etc.)

ELEMENTAL MANIPULATION

Rank: Novice
Power Points: 1
Range: Smarts x 2
Duration: Instant
Trappings: A few simple gestures.

A character who chooses this power must select one particular element to control (though he may choose other elements as a new power). This allows him to perform basic "tricks" within his chosen element.

The specific tasks that may be attempted are listed below.

Air: The caster can create lesser air currents to blow out a candle, fan a flame, lift a skirt, or cool his body in oppressive heat (+1 to a single Fatigue roll caused by heat).

Earth: A wave of the hand can open a one-foot square hole in soft earth (or half that in stone), or cause a spray of sand that might blind an opponent (+1 to a Trick roll).

Fire: The caster can snap his fingers to create a small flame (about the size of a hot match). With existing fire, he can urge it to spread (+1 to see if a fire spreads), cause it

to flare (perhaps as part of a Trick maneuver), or slowly light an object over the course of a few rounds (as if holding a match to it).

Water: The caster can conjure up to a pint of water somewhere within his sight (not "inside" objects or people. A wave of his hand also purifies one gallon of water, whether it be poisoned or simply salt-water. Those who have been poisoned within the last minute also get a second chance to resist any remaining effects.

ENTANGLE

Rank: Novice
Power Points: 2-4
Range: Smarts
Duration: Special
Trappings: Glue bomb, vines, handcuffs, spider webs

This power allows the character to restrain a target with snaking vines, lengths of hair, spider webs, or some other vine-like trapping.

The arcane skill roll is opposed by the target's Agility. Success indicates partial restraint so that the target suffers a –2 penalty to Pace and skills linked to Agility and Strength. A raise restrains the target fully. He cannot move or use any skills linked to Agility or Strength.

Each following round, an *entangled* target may make a Strength or Agility roll to break free. Other characters may also attempt to free the ensnared person by making a Strength roll at –2.

For 2 Power Points *entangle* targets a single opponent. For 4 points it affects everyone in Medium Burst Template.

ENVIRONMENTAL PROTECTION

Rank: Novice
Power Points: 2
Range: Touch
Duration: 1 hour (1/Hour)
Trappings: A mark on the forehead, potions, "gills."

Adventurers sometimes travel beneath the waves, in space, or other hazardous environments.

This power allows the target to breathe, speak, and move at his normal Pace while underwater, in zero-G, a vacuum, in the lava of a volcano or the heat of the sun, the arctic wastes, and so on. Pressure, atmosphere, air, etc, are all provided for the character. Complete protection is offered only for background hazards. A fire attack still causes normal damage even with *environmental protection*, for example.

A success is needed to accomplish the power. With a raise, maintaining the power becomes 1 Power Point per 2 hours (for that particular target).

FEAR

Rank: Novice
Power Points: 2
Range: Smarts x 2
Duration: Instant
Trappings: Gestures, eldritch energy, cold chills.

This power causes the target overwhelming dread and horror. The area of effect is the Large Burst Template. Every creature beneath the template must make a Guts check, apply −2 to the Guts roll if the caster got a raise. Wild Cards who fail roll on the Fear Table. Extras are Panicked instead.

FLY

Rank: Veteran
Power Points: 3/6
Range: Touch
Duration: 3 (1/round)
Trappings: Gusty winds, rings, broomsticks.

Fly allows a character to fly at his basic Pace with a Climb rate of half that number. He may double his Pace by spending twice the number of Power Points.

GREATER HEALING

Rank: Veteran
Power Points: 10/20
Range: Touch
Duration: Instant
Trappings: Laying on hands, touching the victim with a holy symbol, praying, giving a drink of water.

Greater healing restores wounds more than one hour old. This use of the power requires 10 Power Points, and otherwise works exactly like the *healing* power. It can also be used to neutralize poison and disease after the first 10 minutes has passed.

Greater Healing can also heal Permanent Crippling Injuries. This requires an arcane skill roll at −4, 1d6 hours of time, and 20 Power Points. Only one casting is permitted per injury—if it fails, the injury really is permanent.

HEALING

Rank: Novice
Power Points: 3
Range: Touch
Duration: Instant
Trappings: Laying on hands, touching the victim with a holy symbol, prayer.

Healing repairs recent bodily damage. It must be used within the "golden hour," though, for it has no effect on wounds more than one hour old.

For Wild Cards, each use of the *healing* spell removes a wound with a success, and two with a raise. The roll suffers a penalty equal to the victim's wounds (in addition to any the caster might be suffering himself).

For Extras, the GM must first determine if the ally is dead (see **Aftermath**). If so, no *healing* may be attempted. If not, a successful arcane skill roll returns the ally to the game Shaken.

Healing can also cure poison and disease if used within 10 minutes of the event.

INVISIBILITY

Rank: Seasoned
Power Points: 5
Range: Self
Duration: 3 (1/round)
Trappings: Powder, potion, iridescent lights.

Being *invisible* is a powerful aid in combat, and useful for spying on maidens' changing rooms as well. Even inventors and supervillains in pulp genres enjoy the "invisible man" routine.

With a success, the character is transparent, but a vague outline is visible. A character may detect the invisible presence if he has a reason to look and makes a Notice roll at –4. Once detected, he may attack the foe at –4 as well. With a raise, the character is completely invisible. The penalty to Notice or hit him is –6.

In either case, the power affects the character and his personal items. Anything picked up after the power was cast remains visible.

LIGHT

Rank: Novice
Power Points: 1
Range: Touch
Duration: 10 minutes (1/minute)
Trappings: Different colors, floating globes, glowing palms, enchanted staffs.

The ability to create light is a pretty simple one as magical spells and powers go, but a party trapped in the dark with loathsome undead is happy to have an ally with this ability. *Light* must be cast on an inanimate object, such as a coin, a sword, a shield, or even someone's clothing. Clever casters often cast *light* on a foe's clothes or weapon to make him easier to see—ignore any penalties for illumination when attacking such an affected target.

The *light* is as bright as a torch, and provides clear illumination in an area equal to a Large Burst Template.

OBSCURE

Rank: Novice
Power Points: 2
Range: Smarts
Duration: 3 (1/round)
Trappings: Darkness.

This power does exactly what its name implies—creates an area of obscurement equal to a Large Burst Template. Attacks into, out of, or through the area of effect suffer the standard penalty for absolute blindness of –6.

PUPPET

Rank: Veteran
Power Points: 3
Range: Smarts
Duration: 3 (1/round)
Trappings: Glowing eyes, trance-like state, a swaying pocketwatch, voodoo dolls.

Sometimes it pays to persuade others to do your fighting for you. Some do this by blatant mind control, others do it by manufacturing visual and auditory illusions.

Puppet is an opposed roll of the character's arcane skill versus the target's Spirit. The user must score a success and beat the target's roll to gain complete control. The victim will attack friends and even commit suicide, though such acts allow the victim another opposed Spirit roll to break the spell.

Villainous types may have other versions of *puppet* that allow them to control subjects for much longer periods of time—perhaps even permanently. Such versions usually require a personal belonging.

QUICKNESS

Rank: Seasoned
Power Points: 4
Range: Touch
Duration: 3 (2/Round)
Trappings: Blurred motion, hyperactivity.

Super-speedster heroes and the warrior-friends of battle mages are the most frequent recipients of this power. With success, the target has two actions per round instead of the usual one (at no multi-action penalty). With a raise, the recipient gains the benefits above, and can also discard and redraw any initiative cards lower than 8 each round.

SHAPE CHANGE

Rank: Special
Power Points: Special
Range: Self
Duration: 1 minute (1/minute)
Trappings: "Morphing," talismans, tattoos.

Many cultures have legends of shamans or wizards who can take on the shape of animals. This power does just that. This version of the power only allows a user to transform into mundane animals, but more bizarre transmutations may be found.

A character may learn this spell while of Novice rank, but cannot transform into the more powerful creatures until he attains the appropriate rank. The cost in Power Points depends on the type of creature the character wishes to change into. Use the Shape Change Table as a guideline for unlisted creatures.

Weapons and other personal effects are assumed into the animal's form and reappear when the power ends, but other objects are dropped.

While transformed, the character retains his own Smarts, Spirit, and linked skills (though he may not be able to use them since he cannot speak). He gains the animal's Agility and Strength and linked skills, and cannot use most devices. He has no capacity for speech and cannot use powers, though he may continue to maintain powers previously activated. Vigor is the highest of the caster's or the creature's.

The GM has final say on what an animal can and cannot do. A shaman in dog-form might be able to pull the trigger on a shotgun, for instance, but would use a default skill roll of d4–2 as the animal has no Shooting score of its own. The shaman's Persuasion functions normally, but without speech, might suffer a –4 or worse penalty depending on what he tries to accomplish.

SHAPE CHANGE

Cost	Rank	Animal Types
3	Novice	Hawk, rabbit, cat
4	Seasoned	Dog, wolf, deer
5	Veteran	Lion, tiger
6	Heroic	Bear, shark
7	Legendary	Great white shark

SMITE

Rank: Novice
Power Points: 2
Range: Touch
Duration: 3 (1/round)
Trappings: A colored glow, runes, sigils, crackling energy, barbs grow from the blade.

This power is cast on a weapon of some sort. If it's a ranged weapon, it affects one entire magazine, 20 bolts, shells, or arrows, or one full "load" of ammunition (the GM may have to determine the exact quantity for unusual weapons). While the spell is in effect, the weapon's damage is increased by +2, or +4 with a raise.

SPEAK LANGUAGE

Rank: Novice
Power Points: 1
Range: Touch
Duration: 10 minutes (1/10 minutes)
Trappings: Words, pictures, hand motions.

This power allows a character to speak, read, and write a language other than his own. The

language must be of an advanced form—not animalistic. A raise on the arcane skill roll allows the user to project a particular dialect as well.

Speed

Rank: Novice
Power Points: 1
Range: Touch
Duration: 3 (1/round)
Trappings: Blurred motion, "floating," acrobatics.

Warriors who need to close with their foes quickly often use this power, as do those who sometimes need to outrun things Man Was Not Meant to Know.

Speed allows the target of the power to move faster than usual. With a success, the recipient's basic Pace is doubled. With a raise, running becomes a free action, so he may ignore the usual –2 running penalty.

Stun

Rank: Novice
Power Points: 2
Range: 12/24/48
Duration: Special
Trappings: Bolts of energy, stun bombs, sonic booms, burst of blinding light.

Stun shocks those within a Medium Burst Template with concussive force, sound, light, magical energy, or the like.

If the arcane character scores a success, targets within the area of effect must make Vigor rolls or be Shaken. With a raise, victims must make Vigor rolls at –2.

Telekinesis

Rank: Seasoned
Power Points: 5
Range: Smarts
Duration: 3 (1/round)
Trappings: A wave of the hand, magic wand, steely gaze.

Telekinesis is the ability to move a single object or creature (including one's self) with arcane will. The weight a caster can lift is equal to 10 lbs times his Spirit die type, or 50 lbs times his Spirit with a raise.

Lifting Creatures: Living targets may resist with an opposed Spirit roll. If the roll is greater than the caster's skill total, the victim is unaffected. If the creature loses, however, it is lifted as usual and does not get another attempt to break free.

Occasionally a victim might manage to grab onto something solid to prevent itself from being lifted. When this happens, the victim may make an opposed Strength roll versus the caster's arcane skill. If the victim is successful, he manages to grab onto whatever was available and is not moved, bashed, or otherwise affected that round.

Telekinetic Weapons: A caster can use *telekinesis* to wield a weapon. When this occurs, the weapon's Fighting is equal to his arcane skill, and its damage is based on the caster's Spirit instead of his Strength. A sword that does Strength+2 damage, for example, does Spirit+2 when wielded by *telekinesis.* The weapon otherwise functions normally, including granting bonus damage when it strikes with a raise.

Dropping Things: Particularly ruthless characters often use *telekinesis* to drop their foes or bash them into walls and the like. A creature affected by this power can be moved up to the caster's Smarts in inches per turn in any direction. Dropped creatures suffer falling damage as usual.

Victims who are bashed into walls or other solid objects suffer the caster's Spirit+d6 as damage. If a caster with a d12 Spirit smashes an orc into a wall, for example, the orc suffers d12+d6 damage.

TELEPORT

Rank: Seasoned
Power Points: 3+
Range: Special
Duration: Instant
Trappings: A cloud of smoke, "phasing" out, change into a bolt of lightning.

Teleport allows a character to disappear and instantly reappear up to 10" distant for each 3 Power Points spent, or 15" with a raise. This counts as his movement for the round. Adjacent opponents do not get a free attack against the teleporting character. If the hero wishes to teleport somewhere he can't see, he must make a Smarts roll at –2. If it is an unknown area he has never seen the roll is at a –4 penalty.

Failure of either roll means the teleporter hit an object of some sort. He returns where he came from and is Shaken. A roll of 1 on the casting die (regardless of the Wild Die) indicates a more serious disaster—in addition to being Shaken he also suffers 2d6 damage.

The teleporter can never enter a solid space even if he tries. The power instantly returns him to his starting location as above.

Carrying Others: The hero can carry other beings with him, but this automatically causes one level of Fatigue per additional "rider." (More than two may be carried at once, but causes instant Incapacitation.) One Fatigue can be regained for each full hour of rest.

ZOMBIE

Rank: Veteran
Power Points: 3/Corpse
Range: Smarts
Duration: Special
Trappings: Carving symbols on corpses, throwing bones, graveyards, "leather" books.

This power is considered evil in most settings, and so is typically used only by villainous nonplayer characters such as necromancers, evil scientists, dark cultists, and the like.

When cast, *zombie* raises a number of dead specified by the character when he spent his Power Points. The undead are immediately obedient, though perhaps a bit mischievous and literal-minded in their duties.

Corpses aren't summoned by this ability, so there must actually be a supply of bodies available for the power to have any effect. The bodies don't have to be fresh—*zombie* can raise servants that have been waiting patiently for centuries. Graveyards, morgues, and battlefields can all serve this purpose.

With a success, the dead remain animated for 1 hour. With a raise, they remain animated for 1d6 hours. With two raises, they remain animated for an entire day.

Certain powerful necromancers may have improved versions of this power that are cheaper to cast and create permanent undead. The GM has the zombie's statistics.

95

Chapter Five: Situational Rules

We've placed the situational rules—rules for using vehicles, mass battles, and other things that don't come up every game—out of the main section so that you can ignore them until you need them. The vehicle rules, for instance, won't do you much good in a fantasy campaign, and the mass battle rules are pretty useless for a modern day horror game.

If this is your first time through the book, skim over the various sections so you know what's in here, then come back and check them out in detail when you need them.

Mounted Combat

Mounted combat comes up quite often in fantasy settings, Westerns, and even post-holocaust campaigns where humanity is forced to return to beasts of burden. Here are a few notes about how to handle these situations. These rules refer to horses, but apply to camels, weird alien creatures, and so on as well.

Movement

Mounts move on their rider's action card. Even though the animal may move, the rider may still Hold his action. If he's still Holding the action in the next round, move the horse on the rider's Held card.

Falling

Anytime a character is Shaken or suffers a wound while on horseback he must make a Riding roll to stay horsed. If he fails, he falls. If the horse is moving, the rider suffers 2d6 damage (he sustains only 1d6 damage if the horse was still).

Firing on Mounted Targets

Shots directed at mounted characters use the **Innocent Bystander** rules to see if the horse was hit. Of course, an attacker can always aim for the horse instead.

Fighting

Characters who wish to fight from horseback must use the lowest of their Fighting or Riding skills. This makes it important for cavalrymen to actually be able to ride well!

Characters who shoot from an animal suffer a –2 penalty to their Shooting rolls. The Steady Hands Edge negates this penalty.

CHARGING

A rider on a charging horse adds +4 to his damage roll with a successful Fighting attack. To be considered charging, the rider must have moved at least 6" or more in a relatively straight line towards his foe.

TRAINED HORSES

Animals specifically noted as being trained to fight (such as warhorses) may attack any threat to their front during their riders' action. Untrained horses do not fight unless cornered.

SETTING WEAPONS

A weapon with a Reach of 1 or greater can be "set" against a cavalry attack. To do so, the attacker must be on Hold when he is attacked by a charging mount (see above).

If so, he rolls to interrupt as usual, but each combatant adds +2 to his Agility roll for each point of his weapon's reach. The winner attacks first, and adds the +4 charge bonus to his damage; the loser gains no bonus.

WOUNDED MOUNTS

When an animal is Shaken or wounded, it rears or bucks. A rider must make a Riding roll to stay mounted, or suffer the consequences of falling (see above). Mounts which aren't trained in fighting flee in a random direction when Shaken, taking their riders with them.

HORSE, RIDING

Riding horses are medium-sized animals that manage a good compromise between speed and carrying capacity.

Attributes: Agility d8, Smarts d4(A), Spirit d6, Strength d12, Vigor d8

Skills: Fighting d4, Guts d6, Notice d6

Pace: 10; **Parry:** 4; **Toughness:** 8

Special Abilities
- **Fleet Footed:** Horses roll a d8 when running instead of a d6.
- **Kick:** Str.
- **Size +2:** Riding horses weigh between 800 and 1000 pounds.

HORSE, WAR

War horses are large beasts trained for aggression. They are trained to fight with both hooves, either to their front or their rear. In combat, the animal attacks any round its rider doesn't make a trick maneuver of some kind.

Attributes: Agility d6, Smarts d4(A), Spirit d6, Strength d12+2, Vigor d10

Skills: Fighting d8, Guts d8, Notice d6

Pace: 8; **Parry:** 6; **Toughness:** 10

Special Abilities
- **Fleet Footed:** War horses roll a d8 when running instead of a d6.
- **Kick:** Str+d4.
- **Size +3:** Warhorses are large creatures bred for their power and stature.

ALLIES

Allies play a big part in many *Savage Worlds* games. They serve as troops under your hero's command in *Weird War* games, loyal retainers in fantasy settings, or fellow fighters in glorious rebellions against oppression.

Keeping up with allies in *Savage Worlds* is simple. Just download the Ally Sheet from our website and fill in the blanks.

ALLIED PERSONALITIES

You can add a little flavor to your allies by rolling on the Personality Table. Jot down the keyword on the Ally Sheet so that you and your Game Master can have a little insight into each particular ally's character.

For the most part, you should consider these general impressions with no particular game effect. What they can do is help both the players and the GM decide just how an ally might react in a given situation. In a Weird War One game, for instance, a player with a young lieutenant character could look over his list and choose the "Observant" character to pull guard duty. If he has to go with the "Lazy" soldier's for some reason, there's a good chance the GM will rule he falls asleep sometime during his watch.

EXPERIENCE

Allies who take part in battle with their more heroic employers gain experience as well—but not as quickly as player characters. Don't keep track of their experience points—just roll randomly to see if they've "leveled."

At the end of a game session in which the allies had a significant role (usually by participating in combat), roll a d6 for each group of identical troops. On a roll of 5-6, the survivors level up just like player characters. On a failure, they don't.

AMMO

Keeping track of ammo for all your nonplayer character allies can be a real pain. Here's an easy and dramatic way to handle this problem.

The ammo level of each group of allied NPCs starts at Very High, High (the usual level), Low, or Out. A dot for each of these ammunition states can be found on the Ally Sheet.

After each fight, the ammo drops a level (unless the GM feels the allies didn't really use much in that scene). In combat, if the allies are dealt a deuce, their ammo level drops a level *after* that round. This makes for dramatic situations and realistic logistical problems while eliminating a major bookkeeping chore.

Ally Personalities

d20 Roll	Personality	d20 Roll	Personality
1	Young	11	Crude
2	Cruel	12	Agile
3	Old	13	Observant
4	Happy	14	Clueless
5	Experienced	15	Mysterious
6	Gung Ho	16	Creative
7	Lazy	17	Artistic
8	Sneaky	18	Fearless
9	Bright	19	Cowardly
10	Dumb	20	Heroic

Typical Allies

Here are a few typical soldier archetypes you might use for your own *Savage Worlds* games. Fill in any additional skills or Edges as you see fit. A group of rangers, for example, should have the Tracking skill, while cavalrymen should have the Riding skill, and so on.

Soldiers

Attributes: Agility d6, Smarts d4, Spirit d6, Strength d6, Vigor d6
Skills: Fighting d6, Guts d6, Notice d6, Shooting d6, Stealth d4
Pace: 6; **Parry:** 5; **Toughness:** 5

Experienced Soldiers

Attributes: Agility d6, Smarts d6, Spirit d6, Strength d8, Vigor d8
Skills: Fighting d8, Guts d8, Notice d8, Shooting d8, Stealth d6
Pace: 6; **Parry:** 6; **Toughness:** 6
Edges: Any two combat Edges.

FEAR

Certain creatures and horrific scenes may challenge a character's resolve and cause them to make a Guts check when they see them. A success on the Guts check means the character manages to overcome his fear. The effects of a failed Guts roll depend on whether the cause of the roll was grotesque or terrifying in nature.

Fear/Nausea: If the scene was grotesque or horrific, such as a grisly discovery or learning a secret "Man Was Not Meant to Know," the character is Shaken and must make a Vigor roll or suffer severe nausea/mental shock. This inflicts a −1 penalty to all actions for the remainder of the encounter. A natural 1 on the Guts roll (regardless of the Wild Die) causes the victim to roll on the Fright Table as well.

Terror: A terrifying trigger, such as a monstrous creature or unknowable evil, is much more intense, and can rattle even the most stout-hearted hero. Extras are typically Panicked (unless the GM feels like rolling for them on the Fright Table). Wild Cards must roll on the Fright Table should they fail their Guts check (not just if the Guts die comes up a 1). Roll 1d20 and add the monster's Fear penalty to the roll (a −2 adds +2 to the roll).

BECOMING JADED

After encountering a particular type of creature, the character shouldn't have to make Guts checks every time he sees another one in that particular scenario. If the party clears out a dungeon full of zombies, for example, they should only have to roll the first time they encounter them—not in every room. The Game Master might require a roll if the heroes encounter zombies in a particularly different or frightening situation, however, such as if they fall into a pit full of the ravenous creatures. The GM should also enforce a second roll if a new more fearsome type of zombie is encountered further in.

The Game Master should also require Guts checks should the party encounter zombies again in a later adventure, if it's appropriate for his genre.

Example: Buck Savage has already made his Guts check while passing a massive display of shrunken heads in the jungle. When he later finds the chief native clad in a robe of similar heads there's no need for a second check. However when all the eyes open and the mouths start screaming, Buck needs to make another check to keep the cold grip of terror at bay!

Fear Effects

1d20*	Effect
1-4	**Adrenaline Surge:** The hero's "fight" response takes over. He adds +2 to all Trait and damage rolls on his next action.
5-8	**Shaken:** The character is Shaken.
9-12	**Panicked:** The character immediately moves his full Pace plus running die away from the danger and is Shaken.
13-16	**Minor Phobia:** The character gains a Minor Phobia Hindrance somehow associate with the trauma.
17-18	**Major Phobia:** The character gains a Major Phobia Hindrance.
19-20	**The Mark of Fear:** The hero is Shaken and also suffers some cosmetic physical alteration —a white streak forms in the hero's hair, his eyes twitch constantly, or some other minor physical alteration. This reduces his Charisma by 1.
21+	**Heart Attack:** The hero is so overwhelmed with fear that his heart stutters. He becomes Incapacitated and must make a Vigor roll at –2. If successful, he's Shaken and can't attempt to recover for 1d4 rounds. If he fails, he dies in 2d6 rounds. A Healing roll at –4 saves the victim's life, but he remains Incapacitated.

*Add the creature's Guts penalty as a positive number to this roll.

FATIGUE

Heat, cold, hunger, thirst, lack of sleep, and drowning are all sources of "Fatigue," a downward spiral that can lead to a character's death if he doesn't find a way to recover.

A character who falls victim to Fatigue passes through several "fatigue levels" before finally succumbing to them and passing on. These states, and how to recover from them, are described below.

FATIGUED

The hero is tiring quickly. All of his Trait checks suffer a −1 modifier until the source of his fatigue is relieved (see the individual hazard descriptions).

EXHAUSTED

The hero is fading fast and will collapse soon if help is not received. He suffers −2 to all his Trait rolls until the source of his fatigue is relieved.

INCAPACITATED

The character collapses and is near death. He may be able to whisper incoherently, but is otherwise inactive and unable to perform any actions. He can take no actions until he receives treatment for whatever caused the condition.

DEATH

The hero passes on.

MULTIPLE HAZARDS

A character only has one "Fatigue" track. Say a hero hasn't eaten in days and finally becomes Fatigued. He later ventures out into a blizzard and has to roll against the cold. His Fatigue penalty counts against his Vigor roll as usual, but if failed, he becomes Exhausted. He doesn't gain two *different* Fatigue levels. A character without food or water in extreme heat or cold is in great danger of keeling over dead from exposure.

Example: Buck stays up all night on watch for head-hunters as their boat goes down the river. He fails his Vigor roll for getting no sleep and is Fatigued. Later the next day as the boat shoots some rapids he is thrown in. He now must make a Swimming roll at −1 due to his Fatigue. He fails yet again and is now Exhausted even though the Fatigue came from two different sources.

HAZARDS

Below are the most common environmental hazards, with details on when a character must roll, any important modifiers, and how one recovers from any effects he's suffered from it. The Game Master should use these hazards mostly for dramatic purposes. A quick trip to the outhouse through a blizzard isn't worth keeping up with, but a long trek through the Mountains of Dread certainly is, especially if it heightens the drama and makes the party think about things they might otherwise ignore, such as shelter, warm clothing, or eating their mounts to stay alive.

BUMPS AND BRUISES

Characters who suffer minor but troubling injuries, such as being dragged by a horse, stumbling down a slope, or running through a cavern in the dark, can suffer from Fatigue rather than suffering actual wounds.

The GM should usually allow a Vigor roll to avoid damage when suffering conditions like those described above. Those who fail gain a Fatigue level from multiple bumps and bruises.

The Game Master may occasionally allow sure-footed characters to make Agility rolls to avoid this damage instead.

Fatigue gained in this way can lead to Exhaustion, but not to being Incapacitated.

Recovery: Fatigue levels from bumps and bruises automatically improve one step 24 hours after the original injuries were suffered.

> *Example: Buck and Virginia must race down a steep slope to escape the clutches of some angry crocodile cultists. The Game Master decides that Buck and Virginia trip and suffer bumps and bruises if they don't make Agility rolls. Virginia succeeds, but Buck fails, and suffers −1 to all his activities for the next 24 hours.*

COLD

Trudging through deep snow for hours on end, or facing biting, bitter winds, can dehydrate and fatigue a character as quickly as blazing deserts. Every four hours spent in weather below freezing (32°), a character must make a Vigor roll. Failure means the victim gains a Fatigue level. Subtract 1 from the character's Vigor roll for every 20 degrees below freezing.

The standard roll assumes the character is wearing a warm shirt and cloak. If the victim has less substantial clothing, subtract 2 from the roll. Modern winter gear adds +2, and advanced gear (arctic suits) add at least +4 or more depending on the setting.

Recovery: Warmth and shelter from the elements allows a hero to recover a Fatigue level every 30 minutes.

DISEASE & POISON

When a character ingests, contacts, or otherwise suffers from poison or disease, he must make a Vigor roll and subtract any penalties for the poison or disease's strength. If failed, the character suffers whatever effects are described.

Here are few samples for reference:

Anthrax (−4): Death within 2d6 days.

Arsenic (−2): Loss of one die of Vigor in 2d6 days. If this would drop Vigor below d4 then death results. Often used in small doses over time to make detection difficult and mask symptoms.

Black Death (−4): Death within 2d4 days.

Curare (−2): Immediate Exhaustion; death in 2d10+10 minutes.

Cyanide (−4): Death in 3d6+10 seconds. Must be ingested.

TREATING POISON AND DISEASE

If a poison can be treated (some can't), it requires a Healing roll at −2. Snakebites and similar poisons can usually be treated. More sinister poisons, such as cyanide, can only be treated with advanced and specific medicines or magic.

Diseases are much more insidious, and can usually only be treated with specific medicines or magic, and vary greatly depending on the specific malady.

In magical campaigns, the *healing* spell can remove poison with a successful roll minus the poison's modifier (–4 for cyanide, for example).

DROWNING

Water is deadly to those who aren't prepared for it. Here are some standard water hazards and how often a character must make a Swimming roll.

• A character with at least a d4 in Swimming does not have to roll when in calm water.

• In rough water, all characters must make a Swimming roll every minute.

• In white water, the hero is swept into eddies and hydraulics and rolls every round.

• A hero forced to tread water for long periods without a flotation device must roll once every hour.

Each failure adds a Fatigue level. An Incapacitated character dies in a number of rounds equal to half his Vigor. If someone can get to the victim within five minutes of death, he can be resuscitated with a Healing roll at –4.

Subtract 2 from a hero's Swimming rolls if he is trying to hold something up, including another character. Add 2 to the roll if he's wearing a life vest.

Recovery: Once a character is out of the water, he recovers one Fatigue level every five minutes.

FALLING

Falling off a roof is likely to break your hero's arm. Jumping from an airplane without a parachute is certain death.

Falling damage is 1d6 per 10 feet fallen (round up), to maximum of 10d6. If you're playing on the tabletop, treat every 2" as 10' for simplicity.

Snow: Particularly soft ground, such as deep snow, acts as a cushion. Each foot of soft snow reduces damage by one die, to a minimum of 2d6 for falls over 50'. (People have fallen from thousands of feet into deep snow and survived.)

Water: A fall into water reduces the number of dice rolled by half (rounded down), and an Agility roll means the character dives and takes no damage at all, though he is automatically Shaken if he dives from a height of greater than 50'. A fall over 15" (30 yards) requires an Agility roll at –2 to avoid damage.

FIRE

Fire is the most deadly element. Even giants impervious to the puny weapons of sword-slingers burn at fire's cruel touch.

Roll the damage listed below when a character is first burned and at the beginning of each round until he is free of the flame. Only sealed, fire-proof armor adds to a character's Toughness when resisting fire.

Spreading: Anytime something flammable is hit by fire, roll 1d6. On a 6, the target catches fire. Very flammable targets, such as a scarecrow, catch fire on a 4-6. Volatile targets, such as a person soaked in gasoline, catch fire on anything *but* a 1.

Each round after a victim catches fire (at the beginning of his action), roll as if checking to see if the victim catches fire again. If he does, the fire grows in intensity and does its current level +2 in damage that round. This is cumulative to +6.

Smoke Inhalation: Fires in confined areas produce deadly smoke. Every round a character is in such an environment, he must make a Vigor roll. A wet cloth over the face adds +2 to the roll, and a gas mask negates the need for the roll entirely. If the roll is failed, the character gains a Fatigue level.

FIRE DAMAGE

Damage	Description
+2	Burning weapon
1d10	"Spot fire," such as a burning arm or leg
2d10	Campfire, flamethrower
3d10	Lava

HEAT

Intense heat, typically that over 90 degrees Fahrenheit, can cause heat exhaustion and heat stroke, both of which are very dangerous. The actual danger is from dehydration, so well-supplied and conscientious characters can greatly improve their chances in extreme heat simply by carrying a good amount of water and drinking frequently.

When the temperature reaches 90 degrees or more, the GM should pay attention to how much water characters are able to drink. If they are able to drink at least 4 quarts of water a day, they may be tired and sunburned, but are in no immediate danger.

If that amount of water isn't available, characters must make Vigor rolls every four hours. Subtract two from the roll if the hero has half the water he needs, and subtract 4 if he has less than half.

Also subtract 1 from the roll for each additional 5 degrees it is above 90 degrees Fahrenheit.

Add +1 if the hero stops all physical activity.

Add another +1 to the roll if the character can get into substantial shade.

Failure means the character gains one level of Fatigue.

An Incapacitated character suffers heat stroke, and may suffer brain damage. Make a second Vigor roll when the character becomes Incapacitated. If that roll is failed, the victim's Smarts and Strength decrease by one step permanently (to a minimum of d4).

Recovery: A victim who receives water recovers one Fatigue level every hour.

HUNGER

Humans need approximately one pound of food every 24 hours. If sufficient sustenance isn't available, a character begins to suffer from severe hunger.

Starting the first day after the meal was missed, the character must make a Vigor roll. Subtract 2 if the hero has less than half the required amount. Failure means the character gains a Fatigue level.

After the first day, the character must roll for hunger every 12 hours, and thirst every 6 hours.

A successful Survival roll each day provides enough food (and water) for one person and an additional five with a raise.

Recovery: At least a pound of decent food allows a character to recover a Fatigue level every hour.

Radiation

Whenever characters are in a radioactive environment, they must make a Vigor roll every hour spent in low radiation, and every minute in high radiation. Each failure results in a Fatigue level.

Characters suffer no more than Exhaustion from low radiation. Those who would become Incapacitated get radiation sickness instead. He gains the Anemic Hindrance, and must make a Vigor roll once per week ever after or die.

Sleep

Most people need a minimum of six hours sleep every 24 hours. Those who go without aren't likely to be at their best. A character who goes without sleep must make a Vigor roll at a cumulative –2 every 12 hours thereafter. A large amount of coffee, soda, or other stimulant adds +2 to the roll.

Instead of dying, a character who suffers this much Fatigue due to lack of sleep simply falls unconscious for 4d10 hours.

Thirst

An average-sized man requires two quarts of water a day. This requirement is doubled in both very dry conditions (such as the desert) or areas of high humidity (the jungle) as the character perspires constantly and begins to dehydrate.

If enough water isn't available, the hero begins to suffer from dehydration. Starting the first day after the water runs out, the character must make a Vigor roll. Subtract 2 if the hero has less than half the required amount. Failure means the character gains a Fatigue level.

After the first day, the character must make the required Vigor roll every 6 hours.

A successful Survival roll each day provides enough water (and food) for one person, and an additional five with a raise.

Recovery: Two quarts of water allows a character to recover a Fatigue level every hour.

VEHICLE RULES

There's nothing more exciting than a good smash-em-up. From high-speed cops and robber chases through the steep hills of San Francisco to armored combat in World War II or far-flung space empires, vehicles often play a key role in the furious action of our Savage Settings.

These rules are for use with miniatures and the table-top. If you want to run a more abstract chase or dogfight, use the Chase rules in the next section. Vehicular attacks and damage work for both movement systems, and are covered here.

MOVEMENT

The main difference between characters and vehicles is that motorcycles, airplanes, cars, and the like have to worry a bit more about exactly how they move, so we have to regulate movement just a bit.

INITIATIVE

Vehicles move on their driver's action card. Driving consumes the driver's action unless he's stopped, though he may take other actions as well at a standard multi-action penalty. Passengers act on their own initiative as usual.

SPEED

Vehicles have an "Acceleration" value that tells you how many inches per turn they may increase their current speed. A pickup with an Acceleration of 5, for instance, can increase its movement by 5" every action, up to its Top Speed. A vehicle can decrease its speed by twice its Acceleration (or more in a Hard Brake—see the sidebar on Maneuvers).

The player controlling the vehicle decides his speed at the beginning of his action, and moves it that many inches. The vehicle remains at that speed until the driver's next action, so record the current speed somewhere for the next round and in case it hits something.

SPEED KILLS

It's much easier to maneuver a vehicle slowly than it is at high speed. A vehicle moving over 15" a round on the tabletop inflicts a −2 handling penalty on its driver. A vehicle moving over 30" inflicts a −4 penalty.

REVERSE

A vehicle can move up to half its Top Speed in reverse. Driving rolls made while in reverse suffer a −2 modifier.

DIFFICULT GROUND

Slippery gravel, uneven ground, or mud are all difficult ground and work just as for characters on foot. Count each inch moved through such rough terrain as two, and apply a −2 penalty to all Driving rolls made while in rough terrain. Driving through rough terrain

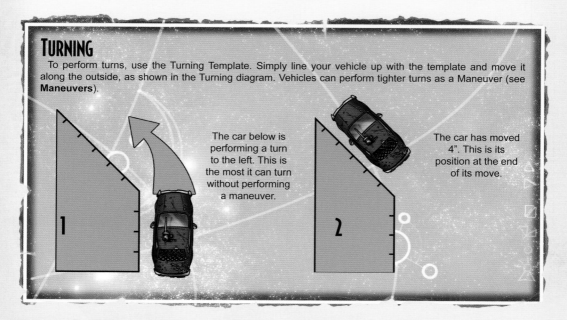

TURNING

To perform turns, use the Turning Template. Simply line your vehicle up with the template and move it along the outside, as shown in the Turning diagram. Vehicles can perform tighter turns as a Maneuver (see **Maneuvers**).

1

The car below is performing a turn to the left. This is the most it can turn without performing a maneuver.

2

The car has moved 4". This is its position at the end of its move.

at over half of Top Speed requires a Driving roll every round.

ANIMALS AND CONVEYANCES

Animals don't have to worry about Acceleration or Top Speed—they simply move their Pace (plus any running roll) each round. Animal-drawn transportation has an Acceleration equal to half the animal's basic Pace. Carts and wagons don't have a Top Speed because the animal simply moves its Pace as usual (plus a running die if it runs).

COLLISIONS

Collisions are very deadly in *Savage Worlds.* The damage to the vehicle and its passengers is 1d6 for every 5" of its current speed (round normally). If a motorcycle moving at 16" per turn hits a tree, for instance, it suffers 3d6 damage, as does its rider and anything it rams into.

Relative Speeds: Increase the damage if a vehicle hits another object moving toward it. This is called "relative speed." If two tanks ram into each other at a speed of 12, for instance, their relative speed is actually 24 and each tank suffers 4d6 damage. Similarly, a vehicle moving away from an attacker subtracts its speed from the ramming vehicle's.

Vehicular Armor: Vehicles with Heavy Armor add their Armor rating as an AP value to their damage.

Safety Harnesses: A seat belt protects anyone wearing it. Roll half the normal damage dice (round down) for these characters. Do the same for air bags, but subtract one additional die of damage as well.

Soft Obstacles: The collision rules assume the vehicle has hit something hard, like another vehicle, rock, wall, and so on. If the obstacle was soft, like a person, the damage is halved for the vehicle. The person takes damage normally, of course.

FALLING OR JUMPING FROM VEHICLES

Characters who fall from a moving vehicle suffer damage just as if they were in a collision. Characters who jump and make an Agility roll suffer half the usual damage dice (round down).

LOSING CONTROL

Failing a Driving roll causes a vehicle to go "out of control." When this happens, roll 2d6 on the Out of Control Table. Resolve any additional movement (such as slips or flips) immediately. Anything in the way gets smashed—check out the collision rules above if that happens.

DAMAGE

Damage that equals or exceeds the vehicle's Toughness forces the driver to make a Driving roll or go Out of Control (roll on the Out of Control Table).

Each raise on the damage roll also inflicts a "wound." Each wound caused to the vehicle inflicts a −1 penalty to the driver's Driving skill rolls until someone repairs the damage. The attacker also scores a critical hit for each wound inflicted, and rolls on the Critical Hit Table to find out exactly what happened.

When a vehicle takes its 4th wound, it is automatically wrecked and the driver must make a Driving roll or go out of control.

VEHICULAR ATTACKS

Combat between vehicles and their crews works much like regular combat, with only a few exceptions. Below are a few modifiers to remember during ranged combat.

ATTACK MODIFIERS

Situation	Bonus/Penalty
Unstable Platform	−2
Fast Targets	−1 per 10" of Speed

Unstable Platform: Any character on an unstable platform, including a moving vehicle, suffers a −2 penalty to any "fine" physical skills such as Fighting and Shooting. This applies to characters who are firing vehicular weapons as well. Note that the Steady Hands Edge eliminates this penalty.

Fast Target: A fast-moving vehicle is more difficult to hit, and subtracts 1 from any attacks directed at it for every full 10" of its speed. This is relative, so a vehicle heading directly toward a character doesn't get the modifier, nor does the modifier apply if the hero is shooting at a vehicle driving parallel to his own.

REPAIRS

Characters may repair their vehicles given sufficient time and at least some basic tools. This requires a Repair roll minus the damage modifier, and takes 1d6 hours per wound level the vehicle has suffered. Field work requires at least a toolbox and basic supplies, and subtracts 2 from the roll. An average garage negates this penalty.

A wrecked vehicle won't run anymore, though its weapons may still be able to fire if they aren't powered by the vehicle's propulsion system.

Wrecked vehicles can also be repaired, but it takes much more time and decent spare parts. The time is equal to 1d6 x 10 hours per wound level repaired. This is usually a Repair roll in a well-equipped shop, or at −4 in the field with at least a toolkit and some minimal supplies.

AIRCRAFT

Aircraft are handled as easily as ground vehicles with one exception—altitude. Aircraft have a Climb score in addition to their Acceleration and Top Speed statistics. This is how many inches high they can climb each round. Aircraft may descend up to two times their Climb score without a maneuver. Steeper dives are covered under the Aerial Maneuvers rules below.

OUT OF CONTROL AT ALTITUDE

When an aircraft goes out of control, it may lose altitude as well. Roll on the table below to see if it changes its height in addition to checking the Out of Control Table.

ALTITUDE CHANGE

2d6	Altitude Change
2	Down 2d10"
3-4	Down 1d10"
5-9	No change
10-12	Up 1d10"

MOVEMENT AND STALLING

Aircraft move just like ground vehicles, but fixed-wing aircraft (airplanes and jets but not helicopters or craft capable of Vertical Take-Off and Landing) can never go below one quarter of their Top Speed while flying or they stall and automatically lose 1d10" of altitude at the end of their movement.

HITTING THE GROUND

Should an aircraft hit the ground while moving forward, it suffers damage normally for its current speed (1d6 per 5" of movement, rounded down). Add in half the number of inches descended that turn when figuring speed as well. A wrecked aircraft plummets 20" toward the ground immediately on being wrecked, then 40" per round afterward. Damage for anyone on board the aircraft when it hits is figured as usual.

CRASH LANDINGS

A pilot can try to save his aircraft—even if it is wrecked—by making a crash landing. This is a Piloting roll at −4. If he makes it, roll on the Out of Control Table to see where the aircraft ends up and halve the damage for the landing. If the roll is failed, the craft takes damage as usual.

Should an aircraft hit the ground and not be wrecked (due to a sudden altitude drop and a low damage roll), finish any movement from the Out of Control Table, then reduce the aircraft's speed to 0.

AERIAL MANEUVERS

Aircraft can perform all of the standard ground maneuvers found on the **Maneuvers** table. Even some that don't make literal sense (a bootlegger reverse, for example), can be adapted to fit an aerial model if you think of it in terms of Immelmanns, scissors, and the like. Aircraft can also perform the following aerial maneuvers:

Stunt (−2): A plane on the table-top that needs to perform a barrel roll, fly through a narrow canyon, storm through a barn, or some other fantastic stunt may appear to move in a straight line, but must actually make important but minute adjustments. All of these efforts require a Piloting roll. Failure means the aircraft goes Out of Control.

Pop-Up (0): Helicopters, VTOLs, and other aircraft capable of hovering can hide behind cover, rise, attack, and then descend again—usually before the stunned enemy can react. This maneuver simply allows the pilot to ascend above an obstacle and then descend again in the same move, so that he's only vulnerable to opponents with Hold actions. It takes a Piloting roll to ascend and fire in time to descend again. If failed, the craft simply stays at its firing altitude or fails to fire—pilot's choice.

Power Dive (0): A pilot can enter a controlled power dive by making a Piloting roll. If failed, he must roll on the Out of Control Table. If successful, he may descend up to 40" per round.

WATERCRAFT

Boats work like ground and air vehicles with only a few important exceptions.

FALLING OUT

Falling out of a boat into the water is nowhere near as dangerous as tumbling onto hard earth. Characters who fall into water at any speed must make a Vigor roll or be Shaken. They must then deal with swimming and drowning at that point, but otherwise suffer no serious damage.

SINKING

A wrecked boat begins to sink immediately. Unless the vessel is cracked open and sinks instantly, this generally takes a little time. Use the guidelines below should it become important.

Small craft (rowboats, canoes) sink at the end of the round in which they're wrecked.

Medium craft, such as a fishing boat, sink in 1d6 minutes.

Large craft, such as a private yacht, sink in 4d6 minutes.

Ships, such as oil tankers, cruise ships, or naval vessels, sink in 2d6 hours.

DRIFTING

A wrecked boat that hasn't sunk drifts with the current (if any). This is typically 2d6" per round for fast-moving rivers, and 1d6" for most other rivers or in strong seas. In the ocean, the GM can roll 1d12 to determine which direction a vessel drifts.

CAPITAL SHIPS

Capital ships are large vessels requiring many crew. This can be anything from a typical age of the sail frigate to a massive galactic battle cruiser. Ships of this size work like all other vehicles with these exceptions.

CONTACT

Very often capital ships spy each other at tremendous ranges. Catching a foe at such ranges with relatively slow-moving craft can sometimes take days.

If one ship is attempting to catch another, the captains make opposed Boating rolls (or Piloting with spaceships and other "flying" vessels). The crew can help by making a group Boating (or other appropriate skill) roll. Each attempt takes about eight hours. If the pursuer wins with a raise he has brought his foe to Close Quarters. If the target wins with a raise he has escaped.

CLOSE QUARTERS

Once ships are in close quarters, the standard chase rules apply (see below). The Range Increment is 50 for age of the sail ships and 100 or more for modern or futuristic vessels.

Older vessels may only fire one-quarter of their weapons at a single target each round. They can however "Cross the T" by succeeding in a Force maneuver within Short Range. This allows the ship to fire up to half its weaponry at the target.

With the advent of the turret modern and futuristic ships don't suffer this penalty.

Roll separately for each weapon using the lowest of the crew's Shooting or Boating. This is *not* a group roll—only the gunner lines up the shot. Characters may fire the cannon as usual of course.

OUT OF CONTROL

When ships go out of control, treat a Roll Over or Flip as a Blast instead. 1d10 random crewmen are lost, either blown overboard or sucked into space.

CRITICAL HITS

Damage against these huge ships works as usual but with a few additional details to any Critical Hits suffered.

Engine: Acceleration and Top Speed drop by one quarter. Age of the sail ships lose one quarter if they have four masts, one third if they have three masts and so on.

Controls: The steering system is hit. The ship may only turn to the left or right, and suffers –2 Handling.

Chassis: Count damage normally but roll 1d6 as well. If the result is a 6, fire has been started (see Fire section).

Crew: Crew Critical Hits inflict 2d6 casualties scattered randomly among all crewmen. Remove that many crew immediately. They may recover after the fight in the normal method.

If the 2d6 roll comes up doubled, a random player character or other named personality was hit as well. Subtract the Armor value of the ship from the damage if the victim was below decks.

Weapon: A single weapon is destroyed.

Wrecked: Unarmed ships begin to sink or hemorrhage air. Vessels with weaponry suffer a direct hit to their central magazine setting off a titanic explosion that destroys the ship and causes 4d6 damage to all named characters. Assume only 10% of the rest of the crew survive.

FIRE

On large ships fire is just as deadly as enemy weapons. Roll 1d6 at the beginning of each round for each fire to see what effect it has on the ship.

FIRE TABLE

d6 Roll	Result
1	The fire burns out.
2-4	The fire continues to burn.
5	The fire causes a wound.
6	The fire spreads, making two fires.

Fighting Fires: A team equal to half the ship's base Toughness (ignore Armor) is required. The team takes one round to assemble, and the next may make a group Boating roll at –2 for one fire. With a success the fire is put out.

OUT OF CONTROL

2d6	Effect
2	**Roll Over:** The vehicle performs a Slip and rolls over 1d6 times in that direction. Roll collision damage for the vehicle and everyone inside. Any exterior-mounted weapons or accessories are ruined.
3-4	**Spin:** Move the vehicle 1d6" in the direction of the maneuver, or 1d6" away from a damaging blow. Roll a d12, read it like a clock facing, and point the vehicle in that direction.
5-9	**Skid:** Move the vehicle 1d4" left or right (in the direction of a failed maneuver, or away from a damaging attack).
10-11	**Slip:** Move the vehicle 1d6" left or right (in the direction of a failed maneuver, or away from a damaging attack).
12	**Flip:** The vehicle flips end over end 1d4 times. Move it forward that many increments of its own length. Roll collision damage for the vehicle, its passengers, and anything it hits. Slow and heavy vehicles such as tanks (GM's discretion) don't flip but suffer a Slip or Skid instead.

CRITICAL HITS

2d6	Effect
2	**Scratch and Dent:** The attack merely scratches the paint. There's no permanent damage.
3	**Engine:** The engine is hit. Oil leaks, pistons misfire, etc. Acceleration is halved (round down). This does not affect deceleration, however.
4	**Locomotion:** The wheels, tracks, or whatever have been hit. Halve the vehicle's Top Speed immediately. If the vehicle is pulled by animals, the shot hits one of them instead.
5	**Controls:** The control system is hit. Until a Repair roll is made, the vehicle can only perform turns to one side (1-3 left, 4-6 right). This may prohibit certain maneuvers as well.
6-8	**Chassis:** The vehicle suffers a hit in the body with no special effects.
9-10	**Crew:** A random crew member is hit. The damage from the attack is rerolled. If the character is inside the vehicle, subtract the vehicle's Armor from the damage. Damage caused by an explosion affects all passengers in the vehicle.
11	**Weapon:** A random weapon on the side of the vehicle that was hit is destroyed and may no longer be used. If there is no weapon, this is a Chassis hit instead.
12	**Wrecked:** The vehicle is wrecked and automatically goes Out of Control.

CHASES

Chases and even massive dogfights with the Savage Worlds rules are fast, furious, and fun just like battles between characters. Use this abstract movement system for long chases or aerial dogfights—not when you're battling it out on the table-top. Note that we use driver and Driving and pilot and Piloting interchangeably, though in the case of a foot race, the characters roll Agility where needed.

SETUP

To start a chase, first get a token of some sort for every plane, spaceship, horse, chariot, runner, or what-have-you in the fight. If the characters are in a large vehicle, you should have them decide where they are within it. In a B-17 for example, everyone should know who is on the left and right waist guns, the ball turret, the nose turret, and the tail turret, as well as who is serving as the pilot, navigator, radioman, and bombardier.

RANGE INCREMENT

Now we need to determine what the "Range Increment" is. You'll see exactly what this means in just a moment, but for now, simply pick the increment that goes with the fastest type of vehicle in your chase.

A World War II dogfight, for instance, has a Range Increment of 10. A chase between a bicycle and a Volvo has a Range Increment of 5.

RANGE INCREMENTS

Type of Chase	Range Increment in Inches
Foot or Bicycle	1
Horse, Car	5
Plane	10
Jet	20
Square Rigger	50
Space Fighters	50
Capital Ships	100
Planetary Defense Fleet	200

INITIATIVE & POSITION

Before taking first actions, determine the vehicles' initial position. At the beginning of the chase, the GM sets the initial distance between the two sides.

- **Close:** 1 Range Increment apart
- **Near:** 2 Range Increments apart
- **Medium:** 3 Range Increments apart
- **Far:** 4 Range Increments apart
- **Extreme:** 5 Range Increments apart

If there are multiple vehicles on a side, they all start in the same position if possible. If the GM determines this is not possible due to some reason, then just move back one Range Increment to accommodate the additional vehicles.

To visualize position, it is recommended to use some kind of markers to represent distance (gaming stones are good). Since distance is relative in a chase, start with the lead vehicle as the baseline and space out ten markers behind it. Then place each other vehicle the appropriate number of markers behind, according to the number of range increments they are apart. Should the lead vehicle get passed, it's very easy to set the new lead vehicle. When a vehicle changes position, just move it up or down the appropriate number of markers.

Initiative works as normal. Every character is dealt his own action cards, and each group of similar Extras receives one card.

At the beginning of their turn, each driver typically makes a Driving roll (or Boating, Piloting, Riding, or Agility, depending on the mode of transportation). This counts as an action for the characters making the roll, and they face multiple action penalties as normal if they do anything else. Various modifiers can affect this roll; see the Chase Modifiers below. A success on this roll allows the character to alter his distance from the opposition by 1 Range Increment (closer or farther as they wish). If they get a raise on the roll, they can alter their distance by 2 Range Increments. Failure indicates no change in position, but a critical failure or any result of a 1 or less due to penalties causes the vehicle to go Out of Control.

If a vehicle moves to the same position as another, they are presumed to be side by side and at most half the normal Range Increment apart.

When moving the lead vehicle ahead of its chasers, it is easiest to move everyone else back instead. This way, the lead vehicle is always shown with ten markers behind it.

Chase Modifiers

The one major influence on success in a chase is obviously speed. If a character has a vehicle with a faster Top Speed (or a higher maximum movement of Pace + Running Die) than all of the opposition, he gains a +1 bonus to his appropriate roll.

If his Top Speed is twice or more the highest of the opposition, he gets a +2 bonus to his roll. Also note that due to the abstract nature of the Chase Rules, characters do not suffer a multiple action penalty for Running—it's inclusive to the Agility roll being made.

In addition, if one side has a lower base Range Increment for their vehicle, then they suffer a −1 penalty per Range Increment below their opposition. This represents the shortcuts and hazards one side faces to keep up with the other.

In addition to these basic modifiers, characters may face additional modifiers based on maneuvers and obstacles as listed below.

Example: Buck is on a bike chasing a car load of cultists. The cultists begin in front of Buck, since he is doing the chasing. On the first round, the GM sees Buck was about 15" from the cultists when he decided to chase them and so starts them 3 Range Increments apart. For initiative, Buck gets a 9 and the cultists a 6. Buck is at a −1 to his roll for having the lower base Range Increment on the bike than the car, and the cultists will get a +2 for having a vehicle over twice as fast as Buck's bike. Buck will need some luck to catch the speeding car.

Escaping

Any vehicle which drops more than 10 Range Increments behind the lead vehicle is assumed to have dropped out of the chase.

If one vehicle has more than 10 Range Increments between themselves and their closest opponent at the end of a turn, they can choose to flee the chase and successfully get away.

116

ATTACKS

Attacks may be made during the vehicle's action as normal. Position may determine which weapons may be fired (vehicles to the rear fire their front-mounted weapons while those to the front may only fire rear-mounted ones). Vehicles in the same position may fire any weapons unless prevented by the Force maneuver.

Vehicle passengers may fire weapons, cast spells, or take other actions as usual. The pilot may drive and fire his vehicle's weapons (or take other actions), but suffers the standard multi-action penalties for doing so.

Damage works as in the table-top vehicle rules with one exception—the driver of a vehicle that goes out of control and Skids, Spins, or Slips simply suffers a –2 to their next Driving roll instead.

SHAKEN DRIVERS

If a driver is Shaken, whether by damage or by a maneuver, his vehicle automatically drops back 2 Range Increments. A successful roll to recover means he takes the Steady maneuver as his only action for the round. With a raise, he may act as normal.

MANEUVERS

Now it's time to start the action! On their turn, each driver may choose any one of the maneuvers listed below in lieu of their standard Driving roll. The maneuvers are specifically broad in scope, and creativity in describing the exact effect is highly recommended.

STUNTS

Sometimes a driver or pilot sees an opportunity to put an opponent at a serious disadvantage. This can only be done if within one Range Increment of the opponent. In the Chase Rules, these maneuvers are called "stunts" and require a Driving roll, which replaces the normal Driving roll for the round.

The goal is to put an opponent into some disadvantageous position, and to do so the hero makes an opposed Driving roll against his target. The following are potential stunts the hero may choose:

Force: The opponent hits a soft obstacle or the equivalent (this can include the attacker's car, which suffers no damage). On a raise, the obstacle is considered hard. This causes normal collision damage. If the drivers tie, their vehicles become locked together. They suffer a –2 penalty to all Driving rolls, and stay connected until one driver can get a raise on their roll.

Distract: The opponent suffers a –2 to his next Driving roll. On a raise, the opponent is Shaken as well.

Parallel: The character can bring any one side of his vehicle right alongside any side of the opponent's vehicle. This automatically moves him to the same position as his opponent. This can have multiple effects. The opponent may not have weapons that can fire from that side (such as from the rear).

In addition, passengers or the driver himself may leap to the foe's vehicle with an Agility roll (at –2 for the driver as a second action). If the roll is failed, the character suffers damage as for falling from the vehicle.

This maneuver also brings the vehicle (or character in the case of a foot race) into melee combat range. A raise on the roll places the character's vehicle in the best position, granting a +1 bonus to the Fighting roll.

PUSH

If a driver wants to change position more than allowed with a normal roll, he can try to push things a bit, either accelerating or braking in a more dangerous fashion. To do so, he makes his Driving roll at an additional –2 penalty. If successful, he gains 1 additional Range Increment to his movement. If he wishes, he may take a –4 penalty instead and gain 2 additional Range Increments to his movement, but this is the maximum that may be attempted.

Putting it All Together

Buck is in an aerial duel through a box canyon with a German Ace. Buck's plane is in the lead by 4 Range Increments. Buck is dealt a Ten, the German a Six. The first round, both pilots decide to hold steady and take a shot at each other. The distance is 10 times the number of Range Increments or 40" this round. Both pilots miss.

The next round, the German goes first and tries to Push his way closer to Buck. He takes a –4 penalty to gain two extra Range Increments and a –2 to attack in the same action. He aces the roll, succeeds, and blasts his foe at a deadly 10"! Buck suffers the damage, makes his Piloting roll to stay in the air, and then makes his own roll to move to the same position as his foe, allowing him to use his forward guns if necessary. Fortunately, he's successful.

The next round, Buck gets a Joker. He goes first and then tries to Force the Ace into a canyon wall by flying straight at the wall and pulling a tight turn at the last minute, forcing his foe to take evasive action. They make opposed Piloting rolls and Buck beats the poor German with a raise, and the foe's plane vanishes in a massive fireball.

Steady

If a driver wishes, he can forego his Driving roll for the round and simply maintain his position. This is often useful when already in a good position, but in addition the driver may take another action, such as an attack, without incurring a multiple action penalty associated with the Driving roll.

Obstacles

Chases rarely take place in flat, level ground. More common are crowded city streets, asteroid fields, and other obstacles to cause your heroes grief. How "sparsely" or "thickly" these obstacles cover the path of your chase is the GM's call.

When a vehicle is dealt a card of the Club suit for initiative, it has encountered an obstacle. The driver must make a Driving roll or smash into it. The roll is modified based on the difficulty of the obstacles as noted on the **Obstacle Table.**

If a driver hits an obstacle, roll a d6. On a 1-3, the object is soft (half damage). A 4-6 means the obstacle is hard. If there are more of one or the other type of obstacle, the GM can apply a +1 (mostly hard obstacles) or –1 (mostly soft obstacles) modifier to the roll to account for the frequency of one over the other. If one type is extremely rare, the GM can increase the modifier to +2 or –2.

When determining the damage for collisions during a chase, figure that a vehicle is traveling at half its Top Speed, and that a character (or mount) is moving at its Basic Pace plus half its Running Die. Then figure collision damage as normal for vehicles.

Obstacle Table

Obstacles	Penalty
Light	0
Sparse	–1
Rough	–2
Thick	–4
Dense	–6

MANEUVERS

The following are common maneuvers that may be performed by ground craft. The penalty to the Driving roll is listed in parentheses. If the maneuver is failed, move the vehicle to the point of the maneuver, then roll on the Out of Control Table to see where it actually ends up.

Bootlegger Reverse (–4): The vehicle moves forward at half its current speed and then turns between 90 and 180 degrees (player's choice). The vehicle instantly decelerates to a complete stop and cannot move further this round.

Hard Brake (0): The driver decelerates up to three times the vehicle's Acceleration.

Jump (0): Ground vehicles can jump a distance equal to one-quarter of their current speed, plus 1d10" with a raise on the Driving roll. They descend one inch for every two inches jumped forward, so a vehicle jumping 20" falls 10" by the end of its jump.

Maneuver (?): This one covers most everything else a driver, rider, or pilot might try to do, such as riding a horse down a steep or slippery hill, avoiding a manhole cover or other obstacle, or driving through an oil slick at high speed. The GM sets the modifier. If the roll is failed, the driver goes out of control as usual.

Obstacle (–2 or more): Driving through a really tight obstacle looks easy enough on the tabletop since a vehicle is simply moved however the player wants. But in "reality," the car is shifting around and is much more difficult to hold steady than the battle mat shows. For this reason, drivers trying to pass through tight obstacles—narrow alleys, other cars, flying under power lines—must make Driving rolls. The standard difficulty is –2, but really tight spots might call for a –4 or greater penalty. If the roll is failed, the vehicle hits the obstacle and suffers collision damage as usual.

Ram (Opposed): Though we have to move vehicles in turns on the table-top, they're actually moving simultaneously in the "real world." For that reason, when one car rams another, we give the defender a chance to get out of the way—even if it's not his turn. When this happens, the two drivers make opposed Driving rolls. If the attacker wins, he's managed to ram his foe and damage is calculated normally. If the defender wins, he must move his vehicle just out of the way, whether backwards, forwards, or sideways.

Sometimes cars run into people as well. In this case, the driver makes an opposed roll against the target's Agility instead.

Tight Turn (0): The vehicle can turn up to 90 degrees.

Two Wheels (–4): Sometimes a character needs to put a wheeled vehicle on its side, maybe to squeeze through a narrow alley or avoid running over some deadly obstacle. Turning a vehicle up on two wheels requires a ramp of some kind—even an embankment can do the trick. The effect is to decrease the width of the car—usually by about 25%. The driver must make a Driving roll at the beginning of each turn he wants to keep the car up on two wheels.

MASS BATTLES

Savage Settings are violent realms where warfare is common. While the game can easily handle dozens of combatants on the tabletop, fighting Waterloo at one-to-one scale isn't really practical. That's what these Mass Battles rules are for. With these you can easily handle a small warband holding a fort against an undead horde, or full divisions of troops fighting a massive field battle.

Follow the steps below to resolve massive conflicts quickly and easily. If you're looking for actual miniatures battles on the table-top, see the free Showdown Rules at www. PEGINC.COM!

STEP ONE: SETUP

This is the hardest part, but once it's done, the rest of the battle goes by like blitzkrieg.

• Give the larger army 10 tokens.

• Divide the troops in the army by 10 to figure out how many troops each token is worth.

• Now give the opposing force a proportionate number of tokens (round up). If one group has 1000 men and another has 600, for example, the larger army has 10 tokens and the smaller one has 6.

• The side with more tokens gets to add the difference to his Battle Rolls (see Step Two).

ADJUSTMENTS

The example above is very simplistic. Very rarely are you able to just look at two opposing forces and instantly realize their ratio. Most armies have a mix of troops of different qualities with different weapons and armor. If you want a really accurate value of an army, you'll have to use the Savage Worlds Troop Builder, available from our website at WWW.PEGINC.COM.

If you're willing to fudge it, you can guesstimate a bit. Maybe each knight in a medieval army is worth two archers or three peasants. Or in a World War II battle, a Sherman tank is worth a squad of 10 grunts, or two bazooka teams.

STEP TWO: MODIFIERS

The GM now adds up any situational modifiers. The most common modifiers are listed on the table below. These are cumulative, so attacking foxholes on hills is a penalty of –2 (–1 for the foxholes, –1 for hills).

CHARACTERS IN MASS BATTLES

The heroes of your campaign aren't likely to sit idly by while war rages around them. Those who want to get involved can dramatically affect the results of the battle.

Have each character make a Fighting, Shooting, or arcane skill roll (their choice) each round. Add or subtract the number of tokens difference between their side and their opponent's as well (if the enemy has 8 tokens and the allies have 5, the heroes must subtract –3).

Also add +1 to the roll for each Rank a hero has above Novice to account for his various abilities.

CHARACTER RESULTS

Failure: The hero is stopped by overwhelming numbers and bad fortune. He suffers 4d6 damage.

Success: The hero fights well and adds +1 to his side's Battle Roll, though he suffers 3d6 damage.

Raise: The hero wreaks havoc, slaying enemy leaders and destroying important assets. He suffers 2d6 damage, but adds +2 to his side's Battle Roll.

Two Raises: The warrior covers himself in glory! Scores of foes fall before him and his success inspires his allies to fight like demons. His efforts add +2 to his side's Battle Roll and he emerges from the fight unscathed.

Ammo: Each round a hero enters the fray and uses his Shooting or an arcane skill (such as Spellcasting), he expends some

BATTLE MODIFIERS

Tokens

+1   The side with more tokens adds +1 for every token he has more than his foe this round.

Artillery or Air Support

+1   Light (mortars)

+2   Medium (artillery on demand, or infrequent but heavy artillery)

+3   Heavy (heavy support on demand)

Terrain

−1   Foe has slight advantage (rolling hills, foxholes)

−2   Foe has minor advantage (high hills, fortifications, trenches)

−3   Foe has major advantage (cliffs, castle)

Battle Plan (Game Master's Call—determined each round)

+/−?   The army gains a penalty or a bonus depending on the tactical decisions made by the leader each round. Springing a hidden flank attack, sending reserves to a crucial front, and so on, all add to the Battle roll.

of his ammunition or Power Points. Arcane types use 2d6 Power Points per round. Characters with ranged weapons use 3d6 shots for ranged weapons (triple that for weapons that usually fire bursts or full-auto). If the hero winds up without any ammo or Power Points she'll have to change tactics for the next round.

STEP THREE: BATTLE ROLLS

Now the generals of each side make Knowledge (Battle) rolls and add all the modifiers they garnered above. Each success and raise causes the other side to lose one token. If the heroes' general is an NPC, have a player make the roll for him

STEP FOUR: MORALE

Each round in which an army loses a token, its leader must check morale. This is a Spirit roll modified by the circumstances below:

MORALE MODIFIERS

Mod	Situation
−1	For each token lost in battle so far
+2	The army is made up predominantly (75% or more) of undead or other fearless drones.
+2	The army is within major fortifications, such as a fortress or prepared positions
+2	The army cannot retreat

With a success, the army fights on and both sides return to Step Two. Failure means the army is defeated but the troops conduct an orderly retreat. Make one more Battle Roll and then end the fight. (A leader may voluntarily choose this option as well.) On a result of 1 or less, the troops rout and the battle is over immediately.

AFTERMATH

When one side routs, retreats, or runs out of tokens, the battle ends and it is time to resolve casualties. Some of the troops lost in the battle can be recovered as they regroup or receive first aid.

Roll 1d6 for each token lost in the fight. The victor recovers a lost token on a roll of 4-6. The loser recovers a lost token on a roll of 5-6. A routed army recovers tokens only on a roll of 6.

Once both sides have figured out how many tokens they lost, remove the casualties from each force. The side that started with the larger army simply multiplies the number of tokens lost by 10%. Losing four tokens, for example, means the entire army suffered 40% casualties. The side with the smaller force must figure out what percentage of his men are left. If he started with 8 tokens and ends up with only 2, for example, he's lost 75% of his force.

Once you've figured the total percentage of casualties to your army, distribute the losses among specific units as evenly as possible.

GAME MASTER'S SECTION

Chapter Six:
Game Mastering

Now you've read the rules and know how to play. And if you're thinking about Game Mastering, you probably have a good idea how to do that as well. Before you start creating brand new worlds for your friends to save—or destroy—let's talk a little about the fine art of Game Mastering.

Your Game

You might think that the first step in starting a new game is finding a group of people to play with. That is important, but that's your next step. Your first step is to get yourself excited. Do that and you'll likely get all your friends excited as well.

Start by figuring out what kind of setting you want to run. What kind of characters might people play? What might a typical adventure be like? Jot down a few notes about what makes your game cool, who the bad guys are, what kinds of magic or other supernatural aspects are present, and what your basic story-line is. If you have these elements, you've got enough information to "sell" your game to your friends and get them to play.

Game Night

Now it's time to recruit. You've got a cool setting and enough information about it to explain it to your friends. The next step is to find out who wants to play, and when they can do it.

When you're finding out who wants to play, first ask *when* each person can make it. It's very important that you set both a time and a regular day to play. If you rely on a fluctuating week-to-week schedule, you're almost certainly doomed to failure. People have busy lives, and as much as everyone involved might love to play, they've still got to study for classes, take care of their children, and otherwise live their lives. If you have a set night every week, it's much easier for your

friends to schedule most of their activities around game night. It also helps you know when you've got to be ready to run.

It's most common for people to play from about 6PM to 11PM on a weeknight, or on a Sunday night. Friday and Saturday are great if you're in college, but difficult for older players who have wives and children as they need their weekend nights to be with their families. If you start at 6PM, your players have time to get off work, grab some food (or share pizza with the group), and get deep into the game by 7 or so.

Make sure you wrap things up by 11PM or so as well. Your players likely have work or classes the next day and you don't want game night to be a stressful experience for them. If you define these things up front, you can help those players with very busy schedules figure out ahead of time whether or not they can handle your game night.

A wise Game Master tries to end each night with a bit of a cliffhanger as well. If your players are talking during the week about what's going to happen next, you've done your job well.

Character Types

Once you've got a few friends interested, it's great if you can give them a little primer information and find out what kind of characters they want to play. You don't need everyone to make characters at this point—character creation is fast enough that they can do it at your first session if you want. But if some of your friends have neat ideas as to their background or basic type (fighter, investigator, etc.), you can start doing more detail work on your story. If you're going to run *Evernight*, for example, and all your friends make combat types, you know they're looking for a high-action, "hack and slash" type game. That doesn't mean you can't mix in lots of other elements—exploration, horror, deep roleplaying, and so on—but every now and then you'll want to have a big nasty combat as well. See below for a little more information on campaign types.

Getting the Party Together

The first thing you need to do in any new adventure or campaign is figure out why the characters are together. There are two common ways to handle this.

The Mission

The most common way of building a party is for an employer to offer a reward for adventurers to complete some task. Perhaps they answer a want ad, are hired in a smoky tavern, or are called on by connections or friends. Either way, the heroes are then thrown together by fate and must learn to work as a team.

There's a problem that sometimes arises from this approach. Say you're running a fantasy campaign, and the mission is to deliver a message to a distant city. But one of the characters in your group is a witch hunter. His player is all excited about making such a unique character, but you need him (and the others) to be a courier for now and accept the assignment to kick off your campaign.

Fortunately, there's an easy way to fix this. Instead of arguing with the player about his character's motivations, let the *player* figure it out. Be honest and tell him that this is what you need to get things started. Maybe the witch hunter is simply between jobs. Or maybe he's working under cover to root out some evil sorceress, or needs to earn some gold to buy better arms and equipment for his task. Or maybe the employer or the recipient is an old friend (or enemy).

This approach not only helps get things moving, but may establish an entirely new and interesting subplot for your campaign!

Former Acquaintances

You can also start a campaign with all the characters already knowing each other. This works great for getting the game moving, and is very appropriate for certain campaign types. *Weird Wars* games in particular, for example, are often best run where the soldiers have served together for a bit and know at least the basic faults and vices of

their companions. This is also a great way to kick off a convention game where your group only has a few hours to play.

The downside of starting a campaign like this is that some players may feel cheated if they put a lot of work into their characters' backgrounds. Players often come up with deep backstories for their heroes. This shows great imagination and enthusiasm for your game and should be encouraged.

Unfortunately, unless you've set the character up as an important figure in your setting and his background figures prominently in the events that are to come, it's very likely all that work will never come to light. The reason why is that individual backgrounds likely aren't part of your overall plot, and characters don't engage in revealing small talk like real people do.

Staying Together

After the first adventure, the players may wonder exactly why their characters might stay together. This is easy if they're employed by a common benefactor, or if similar groups are common to the setting (adventuring crews, military teams, and so on).

Staying together might be more difficult if the campaign goal isn't very clear, or if some of the characters don't get along that well. How to fix this depends a lot on the type of game you're running. If there's a clear, overall objective or overarching storyline, the party might stay together to defeat the greater evil, even if they aren't the best of friends.

If the campaign goal is more ambiguous, the best answer may be to *not* force the heroes to stay together. Consider a modern horror game. The players are thrust together in a haunted mansion for a weekend. Terrible things occur, but eventually at least some of the player characters survive and stagger back into daylight. Why would they then go out hunting vampires or searching for zombies the following week just because they had one incredible encounter?

Maybe they don't. Maybe they all go home and try to forget what happened just like normal folks. Let a few days or weeks of nothing happen (narratively, of course). Later on though, one of the characters gets involved in another creepy encounter. This time out however, he knows at least a few other people who won't laugh at him or throw him in the looney bin, so *he* calls and asks the other player characters for help.

Friction

So what happens if your group doesn't get along? That depends on whether it's the players or the characters who are arguing.

We won't give you advice on how to handle conflicts with your friends. You know them best, and will have to figure out if there are certain friends who just don't fit in your campaign. Remember though that friends are more important than games—even ours. If you and the rest of the group can't talk out your differences, find something else to do for a while that doesn't cause such friction. Maybe you can come back to the game once you've worked things out.

Friction between characters, on the other hand, is not only fine, it's actually encouraged to some degree. Any interesting group of personalities squabble and argue on occasion. As long as this is done in character, it adds to the roleplaying experience and the depth of your campaign. Quiet fights between the heroes can often take on a life of their own, encouraging players to take you, the Game Master, aside or write you private notes about actions their heroes perform away from the prying eyes of others.

Campaign Types

Different groups like different types of games. Some like lots of combat, others prefer to run fast and loose with more roleplaying and less "hack and slash." Most people mix all these elements together. When you cut to the chase, there are basically three campaign types: Hack and Slash, Roleplaying, and Exploration.

HACK AND SLASH

A Hack and Slash game features lots of combat. With *Savage Worlds,* you can do more than pit your five player characters against a couple of orcs and an ogre. You can throw a whole horde at your heroes, and give them a few staunch allies or henchmen to help as well!

The best part is that players who just want to wade into the forces of darkness with two blades slashing can do it. More tactically-minded players can also load up on Leadership Edges and direct the actions of hirelings and allies.

Players who like to think on their feet can take advantage of acrobatic maneuvers and the like to describe their heroes' actions down to the most minute details.

EXPLORATION

Exploring lost cities, finding forgotten treasures, or reclaiming fallen civilizations is always exciting for the players. The Great Unknown lurks behind every pile of toppled columns, and Incredible Treasures await those brave enough to take them from their mysterious guardians.

The trouble with exploration games is that they're often difficult for you, the Game Master, to create. All those incredible surprises, fearsome beasts, and awesome treasures have to be created by you. Fortunately, *Savage Worlds* makes it easy to quickly create just about any creature, magic item, or other surprise you can dream up.

One important tip here. The players don't have access to your creatures' statistics unless you give it to them. If you describe mysterious creatures of different shapes and sizes, don't kill yourself trying to make their statistics vastly different.

ROLEPLAYING

Perhaps the trickiest type of campaign to run is one that involves deep roleplaying. It's very easy to handle rules-wise—there likely won't be much die rolling besides a few Persuasion rolls here and there. The tricky part is handling all the different NPCs and interacting with the player characters. Again, being able to create characters on the fly helps tremendously here. You can jot down a few notes about a character's most important skills and then move on. That way you can concentrate on giving your NPCs more personality and worry less about what their skill level in Pumpkin Carving is.

Another thing to be careful of when running a game that's heavy on roleplaying is making sure there are at least a few events scheduled to give the group something to talk about. If the majority of your adventure is a bunch of people standing in a room, you're likely in for a slow night. If they're in a room trying to find out which one of them is a murderer, the action will likely be quite exciting. And if the lights occasionally go out and another victim turns up dead, the interaction between characters can easily get as exciting as the most knock down, drag out dungeon crawl.

RUNNING THE GAME

Savage Worlds has been designed from the ground up to make the job of the Game Master as easy as possible. The designers and playtesters of this game want to concentrate on playing the game and making incredible and exciting memories. We aren't interested in spending hours before the game creating statistics for Karlos the Innkeeper.

That means that when preparing for your game, you can concentrate on creating intricate plots, tricky puzzles, and interesting characters. You don't have to do complex math to make your nonplayer characters and monsters, and you certainly don't need to spend an hour on some computer program just to make up a few bandits.

Your job is kept easy during the game as well since there's very little bookkeeping. You might have to track a few Wild Card villains' wounds, but other than that, the bad guys are up, Shaken, or removed from play. That means you can focus on describing the action instead of trying to record "2 hit points of damage on the skeleton figure with the chipped paint on his sword."

Take advantage of these things to give yourself a break and run a game like you never have before. If you *want* to spend a lot of time on your campaign, make some cool props or develop your nonplayer characters' personalities and plots—not their game statistics.

INTRODUCING NEW PLAYERS

Getting your friends to try a new game, especially if they're used to one system and don't like to try many others, can be pretty difficult. We recommend downloading the Test Drive rules from our website and giving them to each of your friends. This will show them what *Savage Worlds* is all about and encourage them to try it at least once. If you run one of the free adventures from our site, complete with pregenerated characters, it should be very easy for everyone to jump in,

HORROR

Most every game has an element of horror to it. New Game Masters often ask how to handle horror in their games. They have visions in their heads of their friends sitting around shivering in utter terror as gruesome fiends stalk their underpowered investigators.

Unfortunately, that's not too likely. There may certainly be moments like that, but more likely, your group will be sitting around eating nachos and making bad jokes to each other most of the night. The worst thing you can do is try and stop them. Remember that they're there to have a good time and socialize while exercising their own awesome imaginations. Let them enjoy themselves, and don't try to be overly oppressive with the spooky stuff.

When the time comes and the weirdness begins, subtly change the tone a bit. Smile and dim the lights, then turn on some creepy music—just loud enough for them to hear it without being too overt. If what you're running is genuinely creepy, your group will be relaxed and willing to go with the flow and let the heebie-jeebies take over. Try and *force* them and it will almost certainly backfire.

Whatever you do, when the group finally encounters some horrid monster, make sure to describe it rather than refer to it by name. A "large, lanky, green-skinned creature with drool dripping from its fangs and beady black eyes" is much more frightening than "a troll."

play a short session, and figure out if it's for them. We hope it is of course. If so, you can then try something with a little more meat, such as *Sundered Skies, Slipstream,* or even a world of your own creation. If you like these rules but have a favorite game world, you can convert it over (several of the most popular games and properties are available from our website right now).

LEARNING THE RULES

Before you start a game, at least know and understand the rules in the Test Drive. You need to know how to make Trait rolls, use Wild Dice, attack, and handle wounds. Everything else in this book, from vehicle rules to combat maneuvers, can be ignored until you need it.

EXPERIENCE

You should usually award two experience points per game session. That means your players get to upgrade their characters every other game.

When you end longer adventures, story arcs that take four to six sessions or so, you might want to award three points, but any more should be reserved for really big events. Keeping your average award to two means your characters progress at a more natural rate, and won't be Legendary warriors after only a few months of play.

STARTING WITH EXPERIENCED CHARACTERS

In general, player characters at the start of *Savage Worlds* campaigns are wet-behind-the-ears rookies. They've got a little training and talent, but haven't had many adventures on their own yet.

You may occasionally want to start a campaign with more experienced characters. That's encouraged for really difficult worlds, or for shorter campaigns where the heroes need to get to the heart of the action a little quicker. A commando raid in World War Two, an assault on a liche's lair, or super spies

infiltrating a diabolical villain's base are not adventures for the inexperienced.

We recommend starting experienced characters as Seasoned, or very rarely, Veterans, when first trying this out. Once you have a good feel for more experienced characters, you can go as high as you want.

It's important to the balancing process to make your players create their characters as Novices and then "bump" them up through their four progressions per rank. That maintains a more realistic progression of attributes and skills, and ensures they can't take more advanced Edges than they would otherwise be entitled to.

It's also easier to do it this way from a player's perspective. It's a little tricky to add up all the "points" one would have at Seasoned rank. Bump up a character from a Novice however and the advancement system is a very simple.

BENNIES

Experience is very limited—we encourage you to give out two points just about every game session. Bennies are much more flexible, and allow you to reward creative players on the spot for their actions.

You should hand out a benny anytime a player does something particularly clever, finds a very important clue, or generally advances the plot. You should also hand out bennies for great roleplaying. If a Loyal character jeopardizes his life to save his comrade, he definitely deserves a benny for his efforts. It never hurts to reward a player for a great line, side-splitting in-game joke, or even a rare serious and dramatic moment.

Average players should get one or two extra bennies per night. Really good roleplayers may wind up with two to three.

NPCs

The backbone of any good game is the world that surrounds the player characters, and nonplayer characters are a big part of that. This section shows you how to breathe life into the supporting cast of your world.

CREATING NPCS

Consider this Game Master's Rule #1 when it comes to NPCs: Don't "design" them!

Don't create your NPCs with the character creation rules. Just give them what you think they ought to have in their various skills and attributes and move on. Remember this game is supposed to be easy for you to set up, run, and play. Don't sit around adding up skill points for NPCs when you could be designing fiendish traps and thinking up nasty special abilities for your monsters!

A careful look through the rules notes that you never need to know a character's rank—it's purely a mechanic for balancing player characters so that no one individual dominates the game.

PERSONALITY

Far more important than most nonplayer character's statistics are their personalities. Jot down a note or two about any NPCs the party is likely to come across so you'll have some idea how to run them. Some Game Masters find it useful to identify prominent NPCs with actors or characters from film, television, books, or comics. Knowing that the Captain of the City Guard is "played by Sam Elliot," for instance, gives you a good handle on how to handle interactions with him. He's likely to be gruff, to the point, and have a deep, throaty voice.

Adding these extra touches to the characters can really make them stand out and be remembered by your players as well. That way the Captain becomes a memorable character they may call on in the future rather than just a one-shot resource they forget about by the next scene. Not every NPC needs this kind of depth of course, but those that do add a level of realism and continuity to your game.

Reaction Table

2d6	Initial Reaction
2	**Hostile:** The NPC is openly hostile and does his best to stand in the hero's way. He won't help without an overwhelming reward or payment of some kind.
3-4	**Uncooperative:** The NPC isn't willing to help unless there's a significant advantage to himself.
5-9	**Neutral:** The NPC has no particular attitude, and will help for little reward if the task at hand is very easy. If the task is difficult, he'll require substantial payment of some kind.
10-11	**Friendly:** The NPC will go out of his way for the hero. He'll likely do easy tasks for free (or very little), and is willing to do more dangerous tasks for fair pay or other favors.
12	**Helpful:** The NPC is anxious to help the hero, and will probably do so for little or no pay depending on the nature of the task.

Reactions

These rules are covered in the Game Master's chapter because they only apply to nonplayer characters. Player characters should never roll on this chart. How they want to approach someone is completely up to them and their particular personality. That's why it's called "roleplaying." Each player must make up his mind about how his character reacts to the members of his party. (An NPC's Charisma is a good measure of their likability though.)

For nonplayer characters, you should decide their initial attitudes if you have a strong idea of what it should be. If the heroes work for the City Watch and the NPC is a member of the Thieves Guild, he's likely going to be at least Uncooperative if not openly Hostile.

For those times when you don't have a strong feeling or plan as to how some random character might react to your heroes, however, these rules come in handy.

Persuasion & Streetwise

When a player character asks a nonplayer character to do something, or tries to use the Persuasion or Streetwise skills, roll 2d6 on the table below and add both characters Charisma modifiers to the roll. This is the nonplayer character's initial attitude to the hero. This gives you a good idea of what the NPC is willing to do for the player character, how much it might cost, or what the adventurer might have to do in return.

If the hero says the right thing or offers a significant reward, he may increase his initial reaction a step (though usually only one step per encounter). The opposite is also true.

ALLIES

Though it's rarely written, most games assume that the Game Master controls the nonplayer characters, both when they're being talked to and when they fight alongside the player characters in combat. Most of the time, this means the overworked GM simply forgets about the additional characters during a fight, or shoves them off to the side and narratively describes what happens to them. This goes for hirelings as well as animal companions, sidekicks, or love interests. The simple fact is that in most games, allies are a cumbersome complication.

As great as this works in the game, it can take a little getting used to. If you've been Game Mastering other games for a long time and have a hard time letting go of the nonplayer characters, we suggest you try it for a bit.

The GM acts out these allies when they're spoken to, of course, but he should very rarely, if ever, take them over in combat.

Here are some of the advantages to letting your heroes control allied Nonplayer characters.

First, the players themselves will come to care about their troops. Those extra hands in a fight can really come in handy. In *Savage Worlds,* players quickly come to realize allies are just as precious as new abilities and solid gold goodies. Having a couple of extra sword-swingers when clearing out an orc lair is nice. Using them to help defeat an evil liche's horde is a downright necessity. You'll see your group commit extraordinary acts of courage and heroism just to save a hireling they would ordinarily have forgotten about.

Second, allies allow tactical-minded players to do more than just swing a sword or yank a trigger. Some of the most effective characters in *Savage Worlds* are those who have a number of Leadership Edges and valorous men-at-arms to use them on.

Third, those players who really want pet animals, familiars, and so on really get a unique treat. Like other allies, such companions are usually forgotten in most game systems because they are burdensome to keep up with. In *Savage Worlds,* a "beast master" type character can actually bring his wolf to the fight and have it do some actual good. And should the animal die, he'll very likely feel its loss more since it was actually under his control and not just an oft-forgotten "piece of equipment."

Fourth, allies are important to a lot of stories, but you, the GM, have your hands full handling the game, rules questions, and your own bad guys. If you have to control a bunch of hirelings, you're in for a lot of dice rolling that your players could be doing for you.

Finally, if you allow your heroes to have allies, you can include all the minions your villains should have as well. Picture an ancient liche cornered in his unholy "throne" room. Would he be sitting there alone? No, he'd be surrounded by scores of ghoulish undead. These lesser minions make great complications for your battles, and your players will have fun bashing through them with the NPCs while their heroes battle the liche and his more capable lieutenants.

ARTIFICIAL INFLATION

When running *Savage Worlds,* a lot of Game Masters become extremely enamored with the ally aspect of the game. That's great and it's what we intend, but it also sometimes leads to very large parties of PCs and NPCs, which then demand very large parties of opponents.

It's okay if you do this—the system can handle it—but be warned that a combat with 50+ combatants will take a bit—even with such a fast, furious, and fun system as this. To avoid this kind of "inflation," pay attention to the size of your party and its nonplayer characters, and then remember that you'll need as many foes (if of equivalent power) to fight with them in any decent combat.

CREATING WORLDS

Pinnacle makes several awesome settings that we hope you'll check out, but it's also fun to create your own worlds to play in. The game rules and statistics won't give you any trouble after you've played even a single game, and you probably don't *need* to create a single Edge, Hindrance, or power (though you may want to). That means you can concentrate on what your world is about, what the heroes do there, what kinds of fantastic treasures they might find, and who their opponents are.

THE NAME

It's not necessarily the most important part of the game, but a good name can really help you nail down the theme. *Evernight,* for example, is about a world of perpetual darkness. *Deadlands* has a Western feel, and hints at the underlying horror. You can just guess what *Hell on Earth* is all about.

If you can come up with a good name for your game, it may help everyone instantly realize just what kind of setting it is.

THE GENRE

Your setting should hint at what genre it's in—you shouldn't pick a genre and then try to shoehorn your setting into it. Maybe you want to make a pulp fantasy game that harkens back to the old Robert E. Howard *Conan* stories. You could call that pulp, but most people will think you're talking about Indiana Jones® or the Shadow. Call it fantasy and they'll think you're talking about Tolkien or *Dungeons & Dragons®.*

So how about "pulp fantasy?" That tells your friends that there's not likely to be lots of shining knights on white horses saving princesses. It's more likely to feature cunning rogues outwitting incredibly powerful sorcerers, lost races, forgotten ruins, and savage combat.

Having a genre-description in your head can go a long way toward helping you figure out what kinds of villains should be present, what typical plot-lines might be, and so on.

THE WORLD

Now it's time to design the world itself. Start with the area you expect the heroes to adventure in most of the time. If there's a city that serves as their home base, describe it in a paragraph or two. Is it a shining example of law and order? Or is it a wretched hive of scum and villainy? Now sketch out some of the surrounding areas. Are the "Mountains of Dread" just a few miles away? Or are such places relatively far away from the centers of population.

There are several software programs available to help you do this if you like. Profantasy's *Campaign Cartographer* is very popular, though the learning curve is a bit steep. The nice thing about using a computer program is that it's much easier to make changes should you later decide the Mountains of Dread were just too close. Or perhaps the players themselves can add to the map in exploration campaigns as they discover new areas and lost cities!

Races

A race of super-intelligent titans are simply going to be more powerful in game terms than humans. That's fine if everyone is playing a titan, but if they're not, the GM needs to do a little balancing.

In general, all races get one free major ability of some sort. The perk should be equivalent to an Edge, or a 1 die type raise in a single attribute. Two minor perks, such as low light vision or +1 claws and bite, are also roughly equivalent to an Edge.

Additional perks need to be balanced out with equivalent penalties—unless all the characters are of the same race. Characters of different power levels may be okay with some groups, but most players will resent heroes who are vastly superior to theirs.

Below are some guidelines on what are considered major and minor abilities and penalties.

- **Major Abilities:** +1 Attribute step, a free Edge, +1 to Toughness, +1 to Parry, +10 Power Points, Base Pace of 10, flight, +2 Armor
- **Major Penalties:** A Major Hindrance, −1 Toughness, −1 Parry, Pace of 2 or less.
- **Minor Abilities:** Free d6 in one skill, low-light vision, thermal vision, natural weapons (Str+d4), aquatic, burrowing.
- **Minor Penalties:** Minor Hindrance, Pace of 3 to 5.

Remember that these are general guidelines. The details of your particular setting may have much more of an effect on how valuable certain types of advantages are. Being aquatic in an underwater world, for example, should be a given. Being aquatic in a world where everyone else must use special equipment to go beneath the waves is a minor advantage. If a large part of the campaign takes place underwater however, and most characters don't possess this ability, it's a major advantage.

New Edges & Hindrances

Now comes one of the trickiest parts of the game. You may want to create some new Edges & Hindrances for your setting. First, realize that you *probably* don't have to. What's in this book covers an awful lot of character types.

What you really may want to look at are Professional Edges. These help you create the archetypal characters of your world. A *Savage Worlds* character with the Woodsman Edge, for example, is a "ranger" in most swords and sorcery games.

If there's a particular character type common to your world, this is the way to encourage your group to play them. Let's say you're creating a far-future *Matrix*-type world with vampires, for example, and you want to create one or more Professional Edges for vampire hunters. You could start with something useful but fairly low-powered, let's call it Hunter. These are guys who know the vampires exist and have fought them before. Maybe their special ability is that they never make Guts checks when confronted by vampires. To reflect the fact that they've had to face them before, you set the requirement as Novice, Fighting d8+, and Guts of d8+.

Maybe later on, you create Vampire Hunter. These guys have learned how to stake the bloodsuckers in the heart, and halve penalties for such called shots. Maybe an improved version negates the penalty altogether.

If there's a cardinal rule to Edges, it's that you don't want to grant flat bonuses to combat or arcane skills. It's okay if they only apply in certain situations, but don't give gunslingers +2 to Shooting all the time, or martial artists +2 to Fighting all the time. You'll really throw off the scale of the game if you do that, particularly as they reach higher ranks. You can give them flat bonuses to noncombat skills, but be careful not to stack them too high with those already found in this book.

ADVENTURES

Once you've created a world and the things that exist within it, you need to decide whether your adventures will be scripted, situational, or some mix of the two.

SCRIPTED ADVENTURES

Scripted adventures are more like interactive stories. The players can make choices along the way, but the overall plot advances more or less intact regardless of what they do. Epic stories must sometimes follow this path—it's hard to tell a story if you don't know what chapters are to come. This allows you to tell incredible stories, but also requires more work as you have to plot out each step in the saga.

When running a scripted adventure, try not to make your scenarios *feel* scripted. The group should never feel like they're just observers, going along for the ride no matter what they do. Instead, use the situation, overwhelming opponents, or "down times" to give the group the illusion they control the story more than they really do. In *Evernight*, for example, there's a point where the heroes can do whatever they want for a time. Eventually, however, they are captured by the villains of the tale, and begin the next episode of the story.

SITUATIONAL ADVENTURES

Situational adventures are much easier to run if you're able to think on your feet as you won't have quite as much preparation. In these epic tales, you present a situation of some sort and then just let the heroes deal with it however they choose. Say an evil liche has risen and is creating an army of undead to destroy the living. What do the heroes do about it? Do they hire on with the local militia? Do they try and sneak into the cursed lands to strike down the necromancer himself?

You will need to prepare a few locations, nonplayer characters, and perhaps a few staged encounters ahead of time. You don't want to have to figure out what the liche's lair looks like on the fly, for example. And you might want a few "random" encounters to fill in the gaps between the heroes' actions.

SETTING RULES

Since *Savage Worlds* debuted, fans have created dozens of their own settings, and converted many more from existing games. Over time, the rest of the Savage community has identified a few general rules to help make your job a little easier. We've also figured out how to use our "generic" system while still highlighting the best parts of existing games.

ORIGINAL SETTINGS

When creating your own original setting, start by identifying its core elements. Spend some time writing down just what makes it so special. What are the themes? Is it fantasy? Is science fiction? Is it science fantasy? Is there a hook? If so, what is it? (And we highly recommend you have a hook—there are already solid swords and sorcery realms with elves and dwarves. Try adding something new, like an alien invasion—as we did in *Evernight*.)

Once you have clearly identified the thematic elements that identify your setting, figure out who the heroes are. These "archetypes" are usually the best identifiers of a new world. A husky sergeant with a gruff voice and doomed attitude is a hallmark of Joseph Unger's *Red Rising,* for example.

Next figure out what kind of adventures take place. There's no point detailing the undersea world of Caribdus, for example, if 99% of the action in *50 Fathoms* takes place above water and on ships. Focus your efforts where it's important, then fill in the extra details when they come up.

The last step you should take is creating new powers, Edges, and Hindrances. For the most part, we've found you really want to keep the selection to less than a dozen

powers, and half that number of new Edges or Hindrances. A lot of new Game Masters go crazy creating hundreds of each, but at the end of the day find that most of the stuff people actually take is already covered in the main *Savage Worlds* rule book. That's not to say you shouldn't have some cool new powers, Edges, or Hindrances—just that you should think them through very carefully, and add them mostly for flavor or to cover some very unique feature of the setting that the rules don't currently cover.

Converted Settings

There are literally thousands of great roleplaying settings out there made by other companies besides Great White Games. Don't worry, we're fans of many of these brilliant worlds as well. But we usually like playing them with *Savage Worlds*. Once you get a taste of Fast! Furious! Fun!, it's hard to play a game with an exciting premise but 2nd generation rules. Here are some tips we've learned after a few years of watching folks "savage" other games.

Don't reinvent the wheel. *Savage Worlds* was designed for quick play with minimal rule interference. All too often conversions of other games try to account for every element—massive skill lists, minute details, and hundreds of powers. This isn't *Savage Worlds*, and bringing in those elements is likely to burden the rules to the point where the game play is no longer fast, furious, or fun.

Like an original setting, identify the themes of the other game and try to adapt with a very few key world rules. Literal translations of game mechanics from other systems usually just result in cumbersome sub-systems that don't add one minute of fun to the Savage version.

There is a often a strong desire to create lots of new skills, Edges, and powers to fit your setting. That's understandable, but it isn't always the best path.

Remember that more skills dilutes the

pool from which the players can choose. It weakens the overall character, because now their 15 skill points have to be spread further. Creating a list of 20 different firearm skills might be more realistic, but the system wasn't designed that way and it becomes a major burden to the players. You also have to balance out skill points between someone who's learned how to fire a lot of guns but now can't do anything else, with the character who takes every one type of many skills and never uses the other subskills. Creating one new Edge that allows a person to specialize in a specific gun is a better way to go if that's particularly important to the feel of your game (as it might be in a high-tech military campaign).

Remember too that a lot of what you are looking for is already in the rules. Do you need a sniper Edge? That's Marksman. Do you need a Mechanic skill? Why not use Repair? Do you need a magic missile power? Why not use *bolt*?

A nice trick is to use the concept of trappings and apply it to other elements within the rules, perhaps with small tweaks. Why create a Whirling Dervish Edge when you can just use Berserk to the same effect—renamed of course.

Only as a last resort should you create a new skill, Edge or power. Even then, try to make sure the thing you just created isn't so specific. No need to create Dancing, Oratory, Acting, and Singing Skills, when a single Perform skill will do the trick. Especially if the character forced to take it might use it once in the entire campaign.

And don't forget Hindrances. In the rush to create more cool powers, a well placed new Hindrance can do a lot more for capturing a setting's feel than dozens of new skills or Edges. In an ancient Asian setting, a Peasant Hindrance, with a penalty to use 'Samurai' weapons goes a lot further than breaking the Fighting skill into dozens of parts.

Monsters and NPCs should be considered in real-world terms, then translated into the game. You might be able to come up with a good conversion formula, but if you know a bull dragon in your world is about as strong and tough as an elephant in the real world, just look at the *Savage Worlds* dragon and go from there. That's much easier—and much less confining—than trying to convert every attribute, skill, and hit point.

TRIM THE FAT!

Now that you have your theme and your mechanics are in place, it's time to go back and get rid of the stuff that doesn't fit or isn't needed. Does your fantasy setting really need elves and dwarves? Or did you include them because every fantasy setting since *The Hobbit* has them? Would anything be lost by their removal? Could something else take their place? Do you really need those extensive computer rules in a sci-fi setting? *Star Trek* might need extensive computer rules—*Star Wars* does not. Even then, a Knowledge (Computer Use) skill probably does everything you need.

FINAL NOTE

At all times, remember to keep it FFF. All progress in creating a setting should further the setting's feel, but never at the expense of FFF. These are some of the lessons we think work for most people and most settings, and have been echoed on our forums and listservs since *Savage Worlds* came out in March of 2003. But it's your game, and you need to decide what works best for you.

Chapter Seven: Villains & Monsters

We've talked about heroes and their antics. Now it's time to deal with the monsters, villains, and bad guys. Below are some common abilities available to non-player characters. Game Mastered characters and creatures can also have any regular Edges or Hindrances you feel are appropriate.

One major word of warning before you go any further. Don't create monsters or villains like player characters. Just give them the abilities you want them to have and spend your time and mental energy on better things, like the plot of the game or how best to entertain your group.

MONSTROUS ABILITIES

AQUATIC

The creature is native to the water. It is a natural swimmer and cannot drown. While in the water, its Pace is generally equal to its Swimming skill, but some creatures (usually fish) may have much higher movement rates.

ARMOR

A creature's Armor adds to the creature's Toughness (already added in to its statistics), usually in all locations. Thick, leathery hide generally offers 2 points of Armor. "Armored" creatures like a stegosaurus generally have 4 or more points of protection. Supernatural creatures may have much higher Armor values. A living statue, for example, might have 8 points of Armor or more.

BURROWING

From massive worms to sand-dwelling humanoids, many creatures are able to burrow beneath the earth and move within it. These creatures can tunnel underground and reappear elsewhere for devastating surprise attacks against their foes. The distance a creature can burrow in a turn is written immediately after its Burrow ability. A burrowing creature may tunnel on its action, and may erupt from the ground at any point within its burrowing Pace the same round if desired. It cannot be attacked while beneath the earth unless the attacker has some special means of detecting it and penetrating the intervening dirt.

Burrowing creatures strike by erupting from beneath their opponents and taking them by surprise. When this occurs, the Burrowing creature makes an opposed Stealth roll versus the target's Notice. If the creature wins, it gains +2 to attack and damage that round, or +4 if it gets a raise. If the victim wins and was on Hold, he may try to interrupt the burrower's attack as usual.

CONSTRUCT

Robots, golems, and other animated objects are collectively called "constructs." Some are sentient beings while others are mere automatons following the will of a hidden master.

Whatever their origin or material, such beings have several inherent advantages over creatures of flesh and blood:

- Constructs add +2 when attempting to recover from being Shaken.
- Constructs do not suffer additional damage from called shots (unless otherwise specified in their description).
- Construct Wild Cards never suffer from Wound Modifiers.
- Constructs do not suffer from disease or poison.

ELEMENTAL

Air, earth, fire, and water form the basis of the elemental realms, wherein dwell strange, unfathomable creatures. Below are the benefits of being an elemental.

- Elementals don't suffer additional damage from called shots.
- Elementals are Fearless.
- Elemental Wild Cards never suffer from Wound Modifiers.
- Elementals do not suffer from disease or poison.

ETHEREAL

Ghosts, shadows, will-o-the-wisps, and similar intangible creatures have no form in the physical world (or can turn it on and off at will). They cannot be harmed by physical attacks, and cannot even be seen unless they desire to be. Ethereal creatures are always affected by magical items, weapons, and supernatural powers.

Most ethereal creatures can still affect things in the physical world—throwing objects, wielding ghostly swords, or even pushing heroes down long, dark stairs.

FEAR

Particularly frightening monsters cause Guts checks to all who see them. Some truly terrifying monsters may inflict penalties on Guts checks as well. A creature with Fear −2, for instance, causes those who see it to make their Guts checks at −2. See **Fear** for effects.

FEARLESS

Mindless creatures, some undead, robots, and the like don't suffer from the weaknesses of the mortal mind. Fearless creatures never suffer from Fear effects and cannot be Intimidated (though they may be affected by the Taunt tests of wills).

GARGANTUAN

Gargantuan creatures are those that are at least size 9 or better relative to their normal environment. Classic movie monsters like *Godzilla* or *King Kong* fit into this category.

Gargantuans have Heavy Armor, so they can only be hurt by Heavy Weapons, and all their attacks count as Heavy Weapons as well.

Gargantuan creatures suffer the penalty for being Huge: +4 to ranged attack rolls from man-sized creatures.

These creatures can also bring their immense weight to bear when moving over creatures or obstacles. Add their Size to their Strength roll when doing so, but subtract the Size of their foe as well. Don't add the "size" of vehicles, building, or ships— that's already figured into their Toughness.

Example: Donga, the giant ape of the Red Men in 50 Fathoms, *steps on a giant spider (Size 5). His Strength is d12+12, and his Size is 12, so his base damage when stepping on the spider is d12+24 damage. Subtracting the spider's Size of 5 gives him Str+19 damage. The spider has a Toughness of 11, so it's very likely squished.*

141

If Donga decides to step on a galleon, he ignores its 4 points of Heavy Armor and rolls d12+24 against its base Toughness of 16.

HARDY

Very tough and resilient creatures do not fall from lesser wounds, no matter how many they suffer. A decisive blow is needed to put one of these tenacious creatures down.

If the beast is Shaken, further Shaken results have no further effect—they do not cause a wound.

INFECTION

A vampire's bite, a horrid spider-like creature that injects eggs into its victim's wounds, or even the disease-born scratching of rats are all examples of Infection.

Whenever a character is Shaken or wounded by a creature with Infection, the victim must make a Vigor roll. Modifiers to the roll are listed in the creature's description, as are the effects of failure.

INFRAVISION

Nocturnal beasts often see in the infrared spectrum—meaning they can "see" by detecting heat. Creatures with Infravision halve penalties (round down) for bad lighting when attacking living targets.

Clever characters may figure out ways to mask their heat from such creatures. Smearing cold mud over one's body or wearing special heat-filtering suits generally obscures the target from those with Infravision.

Creatures with Infravision almost always have normal sight as well.

IMMUNITY

Creatures born in fire aren't affected by heat, and a horror made of pure lightning won't suffer from a *bolt* attack with an electrical trapping.

Immunities are always to specific types of attacks, such as fire, cold, electricity, and so on. Such creatures aren't invulnerable (see below), they just ignore damage from the specific attack types named.

INVULNERABILITY

Savage Settings are filled with violent combat, but many often feature desperate puzzle-solving or dark research into unholy horrors as well. To defeat an Invulnerable creature, you'll need a little of both.

Invulnerable creatures can be Shaken, but they can't be wounded by anything but their Weakness (all such creatures have at least one if not more). An ancient dark god given life by misguided cultists, for example, might be immune to mortal weapons, but is vulnerable to shards of stained glass gathered from a church.

LOW LIGHT VISION

Many monsters, and even fantasy races such as elves and dwarves, are typically able to see in all but the blackest darkness. Low light vision ignores penalties for Dim and Dark lighting, allowing the creature to see in all but pitch black conditions.

PARALYSIS

Certain creatures and poisons can instantly paralyze a foe, rendering the victim easy prey for the thing's dark designs or ravenous appetite.

A target who suffers damage or a Shaken result from such a creature must make a Vigor roll or be paralyzed and incapable of any action—even speech—for 2d6 rounds or longer.

POISON

Snakes, venom-coated daggers, and so on inflict their victims with dangerous poison. Poisons are described in more detail in the **Hazards** section.

A creature with the Poison ability typically injects it via a bite or scratch. To do so, the thing must cause at least a Shaken result to the victim, who then makes a Vigor roll modified by the strength of the poison (listed in parentheses after the creature's Poison ability). The effects of failure are described in each creature's description.

REGENERATION

Legend has it that trolls, vampires, and certain other types of legendary creatures can Regenerate damage caused to them.

Regeneration comes in two types: Fast and Slow.

Fast Regeneration means that a wounded creature makes a Vigor roll every round to heal any damage it has sustained—even after it has been "killed." Most creatures with this ability have a Weakness or Vulnerability as well, such as fire. If the creature suffers a wound due to its Weakness or Vulnerability, it may not regenerate it (it may heal naturally, however). Such creatures also add +2 to Spirit rolls made to recover from being Shaken.

Slow Regeneration means the creature won't be suddenly healing itself during a fight, but may recover its wounds quickly between encounters. Slow regenerators make a natural Healing roll once per day.

SIZE

A creature's size has a lot to do with how much damage it can take, so we add a modifier to its Toughness to reflect its tremendous mass. Note that a beast's size has nothing to do with Vigor—even a mighty kraken can catch a cold or tire out.

The Toughness modifiers on the table below represent average specimens of particular species for comparison, but there are always exceptions. Not every Great White has a +4 Toughness bonus. A young specimen might have a +3, while a larger fish might be +5 or even +6. The same is true for humans. Small humans suffer a −1 penalty, while those with the Brawny Edge gain a +1 bonus. Use the table as a baseline when creating your own creatures then adjust for particularly large or smaller versions.

TOUGHNESS MODIFIERS

Mod	Size of a...
−2	Cat, fairy, pixie, large rat, dog
−1	Large dog, bobcat, half-folk, goblin, small human
0	Human
+1	Orc
+2	Bull, gorilla, bear, horse
+3	Ogre, kodiak
+4	Rhino, Great White
+5	Small elephant
+6	Drake, bull elephant
+7	T-Rex, orca
+8	Dragon
+9	Blue whale
+10	Kraken, leviathan

Minimum Toughness: Normal creatures have a minimum Toughness of 2 regardless of modifiers. Only insects and the like have Toughness scores of 1.

SMALL/LARGE/HUGE

Creatures the size of rats or pixies are very difficult to hit, especially when moving. Assuming such a creature is active, attackers subtract 2 from any attack rolls directed at it.

Large creatures, at least the size of a rhino, are somewhat easier to hit. Attackers may add +2 to any attack rolls directed at Large targets.

Truly huge creatures, at least as big as a dragon, are +4 to be hit.

This particular special ability is relative. Two elephants don't get the bonus when fighting each other, but a pixie who joins the fight adds +4 to its roll. If the elephant strikes back, it subtracts 4 from its roll.

STRENGTH

Strength is a Trait, not a special ability, but because very large creatures exceed the normal human range of d4 to d12, you might need a little more information when creating your own creatures.

Creatures of human or lesser Strength should be expressed as a d4 through a d12, as you think appropriate. Stronger creatures, such as gorillas, ogres, and so on, have a d12 plus a bonus. The bonus depends on how strong the creature is and how well it can use that strength in combat. Just as with humans, there is variation within each species, however. A mother gorilla may have a Strength of d12+1, while its much larger mate has a Strength of d12+3.

Here's a quick comparison to help you figure out what strength creatures of your own creation should have.

CREATURE STRENGTH

Creature	Strength
Gorilla, bear, ogre	d12+1 to +3
Rhino, Great White	d12+3 to +6
Elephant, drake, T-rex	d12+5 to +8
Dragon	d12+9 to +12

STUN

A creature with this ability often has an electrical attack, mild toxin, mind lash, or similar trapping. When it successfully hits a character (even if it causes no damage), the victim must make a Vigor roll minus any listed penalties or be Shaken. He cannot attempt to recover from being Shaken for 1d6 rounds.

UNDEAD

Zombies, skeletons, and similar Undead horrors are particularly difficult to destroy. Below are the benefits of being such an abomination.
- Undead add +2 to their basic Toughness.
- Undead add +2 when attempting to recover from being Shaken.
- Undead don't suffer additional damage from called shots.
- Undead Wild Cards never suffer from Wound Modifiers.
- Undead do not suffer from disease or poison.

WALL WALKER

Some creatures have the ability to walk on walls. These creatures only make Climbing rolls in the most adverse and stressful situations—otherwise they automatically walk on vertical or inverted surfaces just as a human walks on the earth.

A Wall Walker's Pace when walking on walls is its standard movement rate. It may run as usual when walking on walls unless the specific creature's text says otherwise.

WEAKNESS

Some creatures suffer additional damage or other effects when attacked by their Weakness. A creature made of ice, for example, might take double damage from fire. A vampire suffers from a Weakness to sunlight, causing it to catch fire and burn when exposed to its rays.

See the creature's description for the particular effects of its Weakness.

Some creatures can only be killed by their Weakness. They may feel pain or even become Shaken from other attack types, but only suffer wounds when struck by their Weakness. A vampire, for instance, ignores wounds from swords and bullets, but suffers damage normally if hit in the heart with a wooden stake.

BESTIARY

Below are a sampling of some common animals and monsters common to many Savage Settings. Note that for some creatures, Smarts is listed relative to the animal world, and is thus followed by an (A) to remind you that this is animal intelligence, not people intelligence, so don't expect a dolphin to drive off in your tank just because it's a *relatively* smart animal.

Creatures with animal intelligence do not typically level-up as Allies—this only happens if the animal is gained via an Edge.

ALLIGATOR/CROCODILE

Alligators and crocs are staples of most pulp-genre adventure games. The statistics here represent an average specimen of either species. Much larger versions are often found in more remote areas.

Attributes: Agility d4, Smarts d4 (A), Spirit d6, Strength d10, Vigor d10
Skills: Fighting d8, Guts d6, Notice d6, Swim d8
Pace: 3; **Parry:** 6; **Toughness:** 9 (2)
Special Abilities
 • **Armor +2:** Thick skins.
 • **Aquatic:** Pace 5
 • **Bite:** Str+d6.
 • **Rollover:** Both gators and crocs are notorious for grasping their prey in their vice-like jaws and rolling over and over with their flailing victims in their mouth. If one of these large amphibians hits with a raise, it causes an extra 2d4 damage to its prey in addition to its regular Strength damage.

BEAR, LARGE

Large bears covers grizzlies, kodiaks, and massive polar bears.
Attributes: Agility d6, Smarts d6 (A), Spirit d8, Strength d12+4, Vigor d12
Skills: Fighting d8, Guts d10, Notice d8, Swim d6
Pace: 8; **Parry:** 6; **Toughness:** 10
Special Abilities
 • **Bear Hug:** Bears don't actually "hug" their victims, but they do attempt to use their

weight to pin their prey and rend it with their claws and teeth. A bear that hits with a raise has pinned his foe. The opponent may only attempt to escape the "hug" on his action, which requires a raise on an opposed Strength roll.
 • **Claws:** Str+d6.
 • **Size +2:** These creatures can stand up to 8' tall and weigh over 1000 pounds.

BULL

Bulls are usually only aggressive toward humans when enraged. Of course, if you're looking up the statistics here, it's probably already seeing red.
Attributes: Agility d6, Smarts d4 (A), Spirit d8, Strength d12+2, Vigor d12
Skills: Fighting d4, Guts d8, Notice d6
Pace: 7; **Parry:** 4; **Toughness:** 10

Special Abilities

- **Horns:** Str+d6.
- **Gore:** Bulls charge maneuver to gore their opponents with their long horns. If they can move at least 6" before attacking, they add +4 to their damage total.
- **Size +2:** Bulls are large creatures.

Dire Wolf

Dire wolves are very large and feral wolves often used by orcs as attack dogs. They may also be found roaming in packs in the deepest, darkest woods.

Attributes: Agility d8, Smarts d4 (A), Spirit d6, Strength d8, Vigor d8
Skills: Guts d8, Fighting d8, Intimidation d8, Notice d6
Pace: 10; **Parry:** 6; **Toughness:** 6
Special Abilities

- **Bite:** Str+d6
- **Go for the Throat:** Wolves instinctively go for an opponent's soft spots. With a raise on its attack roll, it hits the target's most weakly-armored location.
- **Fleet-Footed:** Dire wolves roll d10s instead of d6s when running.

Dog/Wolf

The stats below are for large attack dogs, such as Rottweilers and Doberman Pinschers, as well as wolves, hyenas, and the like.

Attributes: Agility d8, Smarts d6 (A), Spirit d6, Strength d6, Vigor d6
Skills: Fighting d6, Guts d6, Notice d10
Pace: 8; **Parry:** 5; **Toughness:** 4
Special Abilities

- **Bite:** Str+d4.
- **Fleet Footed:** Dogs roll a d10 when running instead of a d6.
- **Go for the Throat:** Dogs instinctively go for an opponent's soft spots. With a raise on its attack roll, it hits the target's most weakly-armored location.
- **Size –1:** Dogs are relatively small.

Drake

Drakes are non-flying dragons with animal intelligence (rather than the more human-like sentience of true dragons). They are much more aggressive in direct combat than their distant cousins, however.

Attributes: Agility d6, Smarts d6 (A), Spirit d10, Strength d12+6, Vigor d12
Skills: Fighting d10, Guts d12, Intimidation d12, Notice d8
Pace: 4; **Parry:** 7; **Toughness:** 17 (4)
Special Abilities

- **Armor +4:** Scaly hide
- **Claws/Bite:** Str+d8.
- **Fear:** Drakes are frightening creatures to behold.
- **Fiery Breath:** Drakes breathe fire using the Cone Template. Every target within this cone may make an Agility roll at –2 to avoid the attack. Those who fail suffer 2d10 damage and must check to see if they catch fire (see **Fire**). A drake may not attack with its claws or bite in the round it breathes fire.
- **Large:** Attackers add +2 to their attack rolls when attacking a drake due to its large size.
- **Size +5:** Drakes are over 20' long from snout to tail, and weigh in at over 3000 pounds.
- **Tail Lash:** A drake can sweep all opponents in its rear facing in a 3" long by 6" wide rectangle. This is a standard Fighting attack, and damage is equal to the creature's Strength –2.

Dragon

Dragons are fire-breathing monsters that bring doom and despair to the villages they ravage. Such creatures should not be fought lightly as they are more than a match for even a party of experienced adventurers. These beasts are quite intelligent as well, and use all of their advantages when confronted by would-be dragon-slayers.

Attributes: Agility d8, Smarts d8, Spirit d10, Strength d12+9, Vigor d12

Skills: Fighting d10, Guts d12, Intimidation d12, Notice d12
Pace: 8; **Parry:** 6; **Toughness:** 20 (4)
Special Abilities
- **Armor +4:** Scaly hide
- **Claws/Bite:** Str+d8.
- **Fear −2:** Anyone who sees a mighty dragon must make a Guts check at −2.
- **Fiery Breath:** Dragons breathe fire using the Cone Template. Every target within this cone may make an Agility roll at −2 to avoid the attack. Those who fail suffer 2d10 damage and must check to see if they catch fire. A dragon may not attack with its claws or bite in the round it breathes fire.
- **Flight:** Dragons have a Flying Pace of 24", with a Climb of 6".
- **Hardy:** The creature does not suffer a wound from being Shaken twice.
- **Huge:** Attackers add +4 to their Fighting or Shooting rolls when attacking a dragon due to its massive size.
- **Improved Frenzy:** If a dragon does not use its Fiery Breath ability, it may make two Fighting attacks with no penalty.
- **Level Headed:** Act on best of two cards.
- **Size +8:** Dragons are massive creatures. This version is over 40' long from nose to tail, and weighs well over 30,000 pounds.
- **Tail Lash:** The dragon can sweep all opponents in its rear facing in a 3" long by 6" wide square. This is a standard Fighting attack, and damage is equal to the dragon's Strength−2.

ELEMENTALS

Elementals are living spirits of earth, fire, water, and air. These are average examples of such creatures. They may be more or less powerful in specific settings.

EARTH ELEMENTAL

Earth elementals manifest as five-foot tall, vaguely man-shaped collections of earth and stone. Though amazingly strong, they are also quite slow and ponderous.
Attributes: Agility d6, Smarts d4, Spirit d6, Strength d12+3, Vigor d10

Skills: Fighting d8
Pace: 4"; **Parry:** 6; **Toughness:** 14 (4)
Special Abilities:
- **Armor +4:** Rocky hide.
- **Bash:** Str+d6.
- **Burrow (10"):** Earth elementals can meld into and out of the ground.
- **Elemental:** No additional damage from called shots; Fearless; Immune to disease and poison.

FIRE ELEMENTAL

Fire elementals appear as man-shaped flame.
Attributes: Agility d12+1, Smarts d8, Spirit d8, Strength d4, Vigor d6
Skills: Climbing d8, Fighting d10, Shooting d8
Pace: 6" Parry: 7 Toughness: 5
Special Abilities:
- **Elemental:** No additional damage from called shots; Fearless; Immune to disease and poison.
- **Invulnerability:** Fire Elementals are immune to all non-magical attacks, but

suffer 1d6 damage when doused in at least a gallon of water, +2 per additional gallon.
- **Fiery Touch:** Str+d6; chance of catching fire.
- **Flame Strike:** Fire elementals can project a searing blast of flame using the Cone Template. Characters within the cone must beat the spirit's Shooting roll with Agility or suffer 2d10 damage, plus the chance of catching fire.

Water Elemental

Water spirits are frothing, man-shaped creatures of water and sea-foam.

Attributes: Agility d8, Smarts d6, Spirit d6, Strength d10, Vigor d10
Skills: Fighting d8
Pace: 6" **Parry:** 6 **Toughness:** 7
Special Abilities:
- **Elemental:** No additional damage from called shots; Fearless; Immune to disease and poison.
- **Invulnerability:** Water elementals are immune to all non-magical attacks except fire. A torch or lantern causes them 1d6 damage but is instantly put out if it hits.
- **Seep:** Water elementals can squeeze through any porous gap as if it were Difficult Ground.
- **Slam:** Str+d6, nonlethal damage.
- **Waterspout:** Water spirits can project a torrent of rushing water. This automatically puts out any normal fires, or 1d6 ship fires. Creatures within the cone must make a Strength roll at –2 or be Shaken.

Air Elemental

Air elementals manifest as sentient whirlwinds.

Attributes: Agility d12, Smarts d6, Spirit d6, Strength d8, Vigor d6
Skills: Fighting d8, Notice d8, Shooting d6
Pace: —; **Parry:** 6; **Toughness:** 5
Special Abilities:
- **Elemental:** No additional damage from called shots; Fearless; Immune to disease and poison.
- **Ethereal:** Air Elementals can maneuver through any non-solid surface. They can seep through the cracks in doors, bubble through water, and rush through sails.
- **Flight:** Air Elementals fly at a rate of 6" with a climb rate of 4". They may not "run."
- **Invulnerability:** Immune to all non-magical attacks except fire.
- **Push:** The air elemental can push a single target 1d6" directly away from the spirit by directing a concentrated blast of air at him. The victim may make a Strength roll against the attack, with each success and raise reducing the amount he's moved by 1".
- **Wind Blast:** Air Elementals can send directed blasts of air at foes using the Cone Template and a Shooting roll. Foes may make an opposed Agility roll to avoid the blast. The damage is 2d6 points of nonlethal damage.
- **Whirlwind:** As long as the air elemental does not move that turn it may attempt to pick up a foe. Make an opposed Strength check and if the air elemental wins then its foe is pulled into the swirling maelstrom of its body. While trapped, the target is at –2 on all rolls including damage, to hit and Strength rolls to free himself. The air elemental cannot move as long as it wants to keep foes trapped inside it form.

Giant Worm

Massive worms tunneling beneath the earth to gobble up unsuspecting adventurers are sometimes found in lonesome flatlands. The things sense vibrations through the earth, hearing a walking person at about 200 yards.

The stats below are for a monster some 50' long.

Attributes: Agility d6, Smarts d6 (A), Spirit d10, Strength d12+10, Vigor d12
Skills: Fighting d6, Guts d8, Notice d10, Stealth d10
Pace: 6; **Parry:** 5; **Toughness:** 22 (4)
Special Abilities
- **Armor +4:** Scaly hide.
- **Bite:** Str+d8.
- **Burrow (20"):** Giant worms can disappear and reappear on the following action anywhere within 20".
- **Hardy:** The creature does not suffer a

wound from being Shaken twice.

- **Huge:** Attackers add +4 to their Fighting or Shooting rolls when attacking a worm due to its size.
- **Size +10:** Giant worms are usually well over 50' long and 10' or more in diameter.
- **Slam:** Giant worms attempt to rise up and crush their prey beneath their massive bodies. This is an opposed roll of the creature's Fighting versus the target's Agility. If the worm wins, the victim suffers 4d6 damage.

GHOST

Spectres, shades, and phantoms sometimes return from death to haunt the living or fulfill some lost goal.

Attributes: Agility d6, Smarts d6, Spirit d10, Strength d6, Vigor d6

Skills: Fighting d6, Intimidate d12+2, Notice d12, Taunt d10, Stealth d12+4, Throwing d12

Pace: 6; **Parry:** 5; **Toughness:** 5

Gear: Thrown objects (Str+d4)

Special Abilities

- **Ethereal:** Ghosts are immaterial and can only be harmed by magical attacks.
- **Fear –2:** Ghosts cause Guts checks at –2 when they let themselves be seen.

GOBLIN

Goblins of myth and legend are far more sinister creatures than some games and fiction portray. In the original tales, they were terrifying creatures that stole into homes in the middle of the night to steal and eat unruly children. The statistics here work for both dark "fairy tale" goblins as well as those found alongside orcs in contemporary roleplaying games.

Attributes: Agility d8, Smarts d6, Spirit d6, Strength d4, Vigor d6

Skills: Climb d6, Fighting d6, Guts d4, Notice d6, Taunt d6, Shooting d8, Stealth d10, Throwing d6, Swim d6

Pace: 5; **Parry:** 5; **Toughness:** 4

Gear: Short spears (Str+d4)

Special Abilities

- **Infravision:** Goblins halve penalties for dark lighting against living targets (round down).
- **Size –1:** Goblins stand 3-4' tall.

HORSE, RIDING

Riding horses are medium-sized animals that manage a good compromise between speed and carrying capacity.

Attributes: Agility d8, Smarts d4 (A), Spirit d6, Strength d12, Vigor d8

Skills: Fighting d4, Guts d6, Notice d6

Pace: 10; **Parry:** 4; **Toughness:** 8

Special Abilities

- **Fleet Footed:** Horses roll a d8 when running instead of a d6.
- **Kick:** Str.
- **Size +2:** Riding horses weigh between 800 and 1000 pounds.

HORSE, WAR

War horses are large beasts trained for aggression. They are trained to fight with both hooves, either to their front or their rear. In combat, the animal attacks any round its rider doesn't make a trick maneuver of some kind.

Attributes: Agility d6, Smarts d4 (A), Spirit d6, Strength d12+2, Vigor d10
Skills: Fighting d8, Guts d8, Notice d6
Pace: 8; **Parry:** 6; **Toughness:** 10
Special Abilities

- **Fleet Footed:** War horses roll a d8 when running instead of a d6.
- **Kick:** Str+d4.
- **Size +3:** Warhorses are large creatures bred for their power ad stature.

LICHE

Perhaps the most diabolical creature in any fantasy land is the liche—a necromancer so consumed with the black arts that he eventually becomes undead himself.

Attributes: Agility d6, Smarts d12+2, Spirit d10, Strength d10, Vigor d10
Skills: Fighting d8, Guts d12, Intimidation d12, Knowledge (occult) d12+2, Notice d10, Spellcasting d12
Pace: 6; **Parry:** 6; **Toughness:** 15 (6)
Gear: Magical armor (+6), other magical items
Special Abilities

- **Death Touch:** Liches drain the lives of those around them with a touch. Instead of a normal attack, a liche may make a touch attack. Every raise on its Fighting roll automatically inflicts one wound to its target.
- **Spells:** Liches have 50 Power Points and know most every spell available.
- **Undead:** +2 Toughness. +2 to recover from being Shaken. Called shots do no extra damage.
- **Zombie:** Liches are necromancers first and foremost. The undead they raise through the *zombie* spell are permanent, so they are usually surrounded by 4d10 skeletons or zombies as they choose. Some liches have entire armies of the undead at their disposal.

LION

The kings of the jungle are fierce predators, particularly in open grassland where their prey cannot seek refuge.

Attributes: Agility d8, Smarts d6 (A), Spirit d10, Strength d12, Vigor d8
Skills: Fighting d8, Guts d10, Notice d8
Pace: 8; **Parry:** 6; **Toughness:** 8
Special Abilities

- **Bite or Claw:** Str +d6.
- **Improved Frenzy:** Lions may make two Fighting attacks each action at no penalty.
- **Low Light Vision:** Lions ignore penalties for Dim and Dark lighting.
- **Pounce:** Lions often pounce on their prey to best bring their mass and claws to bear. It can leap 1d6" to gain +4 to its attack and damage. Its Parry is reduced by –2 until its next action when performing the maneuver however.
- **Size +2:** Male lions can weigh over 500 pounds.

MECH (SENTINEL)

The stats below are for a 12' high mechanized sentinel such as might be found in a typical hard sci-fi campaign. This is a light patrol-style platform with reasonable

KOCHAKJI

intelligence, a sensor package, and high manueverability.

Larger mechs outfitted for battle have substantially more armor, are larger, and have more specialized weaponry.

Attributes: Agility d4, Smarts d6, Spirit d4, Strength d6, Vigor d8

Skills: Fighting d6, Notice d10, Shooting d8

Pace: 10; **Parry:** 5;

Toughness: 10

Gear: Varies, but typically a machine gun or flamer of some sort.

Special Abilities
- **Armor +4**
- **Construct:** +2 to recover from being Shaken. Called shots do no extra damage. Do not suffer from disease or poison.
- **Fearless:** Mechs are immune to fear and Intimidation, but may be smart enough to react to fear-causing situations appropriately.
- **Sensors:** Sentinel mechs are equipped with sensor packages that halve penalties for darkness, can detect sounds or record conversations via directional microphones.

MINOTAUR

Minotaurs stand over 7' feet tall and have massive, bull-like heads and horns. In many fantasy worlds, they are used as guardians of labyrinths. In others, they are simply another race of creatures occupying a fantastically savage setting. In all cases, they are fierce beasts eager for battle and the taste of their opponents' flesh.

Attributes: Agility d8, Smarts d6, Spirit d8, Strength d12+2, Vigor d12

Skills: Fighting d10, Guts d12, Intimidation d12, Notice d10, Throwing d6

Pace: 8; **Parry:** 8; **Toughness:** 11 (1)

Gear: Leather armor (+1), spear (Str+d6, Reach of 1)

Special Abilities
- **Horns:** Str+d4.
- **Fleet-Footed:** Minotaurs roll d10s instead of d6s when running.
- **Gore:** Minotaurs use this maneuver to gore their opponents with their horns. If they can charge at least 6" before attacking, they add +4 to their damage total.
- **Size +2:** Minotaurs stand over 7' tall.

MULE

Mules are a cross between a donkey and a horse, and are usually used to haul heavy goods or pull wagons.

Like any good pet, the GM should feel free to give the mule a little personality. The expression "stubborn as a mule" certainly comes to mind.

Attributes: Agility d4, Smarts d4 (A), Spirit d6, Strength d8, Vigor d8

Skills: Guts d6, Notice d4

Pace: 6; **Parry:** 2; **Toughness:** 8

Special Abilities
- **Fleet-Footed:** Mules roll d8 instead of d6.
- **Kick:** Str.
- **Ornery:** Mules are contrary creatures. Characters must subtract 1 from their Riding rolls when riding them.
- **Size +2:** Mules are stocky creatures weighing up to 1000 pounds.

ORC

Orcs are savage, green-skinned humanoids with pig-like features, including snouts and sometimes even tusks. They have foul temperaments, and rarely take prisoners.

Attributes: Agility d6, Smarts d4, Spirit d6, Strength d8, Vigor d8

Skills: Fighting d6, Guts d8, Intimidation d8, Notice d6, Shooting d6, Stealth d6, Throwing d6

Pace: 6; **Parry:** 5; **Toughness:** 8 (1)

Gear: Leather armor (+1), short sword (Str+d6)

Special Abilities
- **Size +1:** Orcs are slightly larger than humans.
- **Infravision:** Half penalty for poor light vs heat-producing targets.

ORC, CHIEFTAIN

The leader of small orc clans is always the most deadly brute in the bunch. Orc chieftains generally have a magical item or two in settings where such things are relatively common (most "swords and sorcery" worlds).

Attributes: Agility d8, Smarts d6, Spirit d6, Strength d10, Vigor d10

Skills: Fighting d12, Guts d8, Intimidation d10, Notice d6, Shooting d8, Stealth d6, Throwing d8

Pace: 6; **Parry:** 8; **Toughness:** 11 (3)

Gear: Plate chestplate (+3), chain arms and legs (+2), battle axe (Str+d10)

Special Abilities
- **Infravision:** Half penalty for poor light vs heat-producing targets.
- **Size +1:** Orcs are slightly larger than humans.
- **Sweep:** May attack all adjacent foes at –2 penalty.

OGRE

Ogres are kin to orcs and lesser giants. They are often taken in by orc clans, who respect the dumb brutes for their savagery and strength. Orcs often pit their "pet" ogres in savage combats against their rivals' ogres.

Attributes: Agility d6, Smarts d4, Spirit d6, Strength d12+3, Vigor d12

Skills: Guts d8, Fighting d8, Intimidation d8, Notice d4, Throwing d6

Pace: 7; **Parry:** 6; **Toughness:** 11 (1)

Gear: Thick hides (+1), massive club (Str+d8)

Special Abilities
- **Size +3:** Most ogres are over 8' tall with pot-bellies and massive arms and legs.
- **Sweep:** May attack all adjacent foes at –2.

SHARK, GREAT WHITE

These statistics cover Great Whites, 18 to 25 feet long. Larger specimens surely exist.

Attributes: Agility d8, Smarts d4 (A), Spirit d8, Strength d12+4, Vigor d12

Skills: Fighting d10, Guts d8, Notice d12, Swim d10

Pace: —; **Parry:** 7; **Toughness:** 12

Special Abilities
- **Aquatic:** Pace 10.
- **Bite:** Str+d8.
- **Hardy:** The creature does not suffer a wound from being Shaken twice.
- **Large:** Attackers add +2 to their attack rolls when attacking a Great White due to its large size.
- **Size +4:** Great Whites can grow up to 25' in length.

SHARK, MEDIUM MANEATER

These statistics cover most medium-sized mankillers, such as tiger sharks and bulls.
Attributes: Agility d8, Smarts d4 (A), Spirit d6, Strength d8, Vigor d6
Skills: Fighting d8, Guts d6, Notice d12, Swim d10
Pace: —; **Parry:** 6; **Toughness:** 5
Special Abilities
- **Aquatic:** Pace 10.
- **Bite:** Str+d6.

SKELETON

The skin has already rotted from these risen dead, leaving them slightly quicker than their flesh-laden zombie counterparts. They are often found swarming in vile necromancer's legions.
Attributes: Agility d8, Smarts d4, Spirit d4, Strength d6, Vigor d6
Skills: Fighting d6, Intimidation d6, Notice d4, Shooting d6
Pace: 7; **Parry:** 5; **Toughness:** 7
Gear: Varies
Special Abilities
- **Bony Claws:** Str+d4.
- **Fearless:** Skeletons are immune to fear and Intimidation.
- **Undead:** +2 Toughness. +2 to recover from being Shaken. Called shots do no extra damage.

SNAKE, CONSTRICTOR

Pythons, boa constrictors, and other snakes over 15' long are rarely deadly to man in the real world because they aren't particularly aggressive toward such large prey. In games, however, such snakes might be provoked, drugged, or just plain mean.
Attributes: Agility d4, Smarts d4 (A), Spirit d8, Strength d6, Vigor d6
Skills: Fighting d6, Guts d6, Notice d10
Pace: 4; **Parry:** 5; **Toughness:** 5
Special Abilities
- **Bite:** Str.
- **Constrict:** Large constrictors have very little chance of entangling active man-sized prey in the real world—they must attack while their victim is sleeping, stunned, paralyzed, and so on. Constrictors in pulp and other fantastic genres might be far more deadly. These creatures bite when they succeed at a Fighting roll, and entangle when they succeed with a raise. The round they entangle and each round thereafter, they cause damage to their prey equal to Str+d6. The prey may attempt to escape on his action by getting a raise on an opposed Strength roll.

SNAKE, VENOMOUS

Here are the stats for Taipans (Australian brown snakes), cobras, and similar medium-sized snakes with extremely deadly poison.
Attributes: Agility d8, Smarts d4 (A), Spirit d6, Strength d4, Vigor d4
Skills: Fighting d8, Guts d6, Notice d12
Pace: 4; **Parry:** 6; **Toughness:** 2
Natural Tools: Bite (Str)
Special Abilities
- **Poison:** Snakes this size do little serious damage with their bite, but may inject deadly venom. A character bitten by a rattlesnake or similar viper must make a Vigor roll at −2. With success, the bite area swells and becomes numb. The victim becomes Exhausted until healed. With a failure, the victim becomes Incapacitated and must make a second Vigor roll or die. More deadly snakes (cobra, Australian fierce snake, etc), cause death if the Vigor roll is failed. A few such snakes cause death in 2d6 rounds. Death in 2d6 minutes is more common, but a few take 2d6 hours to kill a full-grown man.

- **Quick:** Snakes are notoriously fast. They may discard action cards of 5 or lower and draw another. They must keep the replacement card, however.
- **Size –2:** Most venomous snakes are 4-6' in length, but only a few inches thick.
- **Small:** Anyone attacking a snake must subtract 2 from his attack rolls.

SPIDER, GIANT

Giant spiders live in nests of 1d6+2 arachnids, but they frequently go hunting when prey is scarce. Their lairs are littered with the bones and treasures of their victims.

Attributes: Agility d10, Smarts d4 (A), Spirit d6, Strength d10, Vigor d6
Skills: Climbing d12+2, Fighting d8, Guts d6, Intimidation d10, Notice d8, Shooting d10, Stealth d10
Pace: 8; **Parry:** 6; **Toughness:** 5
Special Abilities:
- **Bite:** Str+d4.
- **Poison (–4):** The bite of the spider causes instant paralysis for those who fail their Vigor roll. It lasts for 2d6 minutes.
- **Webbing:** The spiders can cast webs from

their thorax that are the size of Small Burst Templates. This is a Shooting roll with a range of 3/6/12. Anything in the web must cut or break their way free (Toughness 7). Webbed characters can still fight, but all physical actions are at –4.

SWARM

Sometimes the most deadly foes come in the smallest packages. The swarm described below can be of most anything—from biting ants to stinging wasps to filthy rats.

The swarm is treated just like a creature. When it is wounded, the swarm is effectively dispersed. Swarms cover an area equal to a Medium Burst Template and attack everyone within every round.

Attributes: Agility d10, Smarts d4 (A), Spirit d12, Strength d8, Vigor d10
Skills: Notice d6
Pace: 10; **Parry:** 4; **Toughness:** 7
Special Abilities
- **Bite or Sting:** Swarms inflict hundreds of tiny bites every round to their victims, hitting automatically and causing 2d4 damage to everyone in the template. Damage is applied to the least armored location (victims in completely sealed suits are immune).
- **Split:** Some swarms are clever enough to split into two smaller swarms (Small Burst Templates) should their foes split up. The Toughness of these smaller swarms is lowered by –2 (to 5 each).
- **Swarm:** Parry +2; Because the swarm is composed of scores, hundreds, or thousands of creatures, cutting and piercing weapons do no real damage. Area-effect weapons work normally, and a character can stomp to inflict his damage in Strength each round. Swarms are usually foiled by jumping in water (unless they are aquatic pests, such as piranha).

TROLL

Trolls in myths and legends were horrid, flesh-eating creatures who lived in deep woods, beneath bridges, or in hidden mountain caves. In modern games and fiction, the ability to regenerate damage and a weakness to fire have been added. These statistics reflect both backgrounds.

Attributes: Agility d6, Smarts d4, Spirit d6, Strength d12+2, Vigor d10
Skills: Fighting d8, Guts d10, Intimidation d10, Notice d6, Swim d6, Throwing d6
Pace: 7; **Parry:** 6; **Toughness:** 10 (1)
Gear: Spiked clubs (Str+d8)
- **Armor +1:** Rubbery hide.
- **Claws:** Str+d4.
- **Improved Sweep:** May attack all adjacent foes.
- **Fast Regeneration:** Trolls may attempt a natural healing roll every round unless their wounds were caused by fire or flame.
- **Size +2:** Trolls are tall, lanky creatures over 8' tall.

VAMPIRE, ANCIENT

Blood-drinkers of lore are common in many fantasy games. The statistics below are for a vampire somewhat below the legendary Dracula, but far above those bloodsuckers fresh from the grave (detailed next). The abilities listed below are standard—the GM may want to add other Edges as befits the vampire's previous lifestyle.

Attributes: Agility d8, Smarts d10, Spirit d10, Strength d12+3, Vigor d12
Skills: Fighting d10, Guts d10, Intimidation d12, Notice d8, Shooting d8, Swim d8, Throwing d8
Pace: 6; **Parry:** 7; **Toughness:** 10
Special Abilities
- **Change Form:** As an action, a vampire can change into a wolf or bat with a Smarts roll at −2. Changing back into humanoid form requires a Smarts roll.
- **Charm:** Vampires can use the Puppet power on the opposite sex

using their Smarts as their arcane skill. They can cast and maintain the power indefinitely, but may only affect one target at a time.
- **Children of the Night:** Ancient vampires have the ability to summon and control wolves or rats. This requires an action and a Smarts roll at −2. If successful, 1d6 wolves or 1d6 swarms of rats (see Swarm) come from the surrounding wilds in 1d6+2 rounds.
- **Claws:** Str +d4.
- **Improved Frenzy:** Vampires may make two attacks per round without penalty.
- **Invulnerability:** Vampires can only be harmed by their Weaknesses. They may be Shaken by other attacks, but never wounded.
- **Level Headed:** Vampires act on the best of two cards.
- **Mist:** Greater vampires have the ability to turn into mist. This requires an action and a Smarts roll at −2.
- **Sire:** Anyone slain by a vampire has a 50% chance of rising as a vampire themselves in 1d4 days.
- **Undead:** +2 Toughness. +2 to recover from being Shaken. Called shots do no extra damage (except to the heart—see below). No wound penalties.
- **Weakness (Sunlight):** Vampires catch fire if any part of their skin is exposed to

Skills: Fighting d8, Guts d8, Intimidation d8, Notice d6, Shooting d6, Swim d8, Throwing d6

Pace: 6; **Parry:** 6; **Toughness:** 9

Special Abilities

- **Claws:** Str +d4.
- **Frenzy:** Vampires can make two attacks per round with a −2 penalty to each attack.
- **Level Headed:** Vampires act on the best of two cards.
- **Invulnerability:** Vampires can only be harmed by their Weaknesses. They may be Shaken by other attacks, but never wounded.
- **Sire:** Anyone slain by a vampire has a 50% chance of rising as a vampire themselves in 1d4 days.
- **Undead:** +2 Toughness. +2 to recover from being Shaken. Called shots do no extra damage (except to the heart—see below).
- **Weakness (Sunlight):** Vampires catch fire if any part of their skin is exposed to direct sunlight. After that they suffer 2d10 damage per round until they are dust. Armor does not protect.
- **Weakness (Holy Symbol):** A character with a holy symbol may keep a vampire at bay by displaying a holy symbol. A vampire who wants to directly attack the victim must beat her in an opposed test of Spirits.
- **Weakness (Holy Water):** A vampire sprinkled with holy water is Fatigued. If immersed, he combusts as if it were direct sunlight (see above).
- **Weakness (Invitation Only):** Vampires cannot enter a private dwelling without being invited. They may enter public domains as they please.
- **Weakness (Stake Through the Heart):** A vampire hit with a called shot to the heart (−4) must make a Vigor roll versus the damage. If successful, it takes damage normally. If it fails, it disintegrates to dust.

direct sunlight. After that they suffer 2d10 damage per round until they are dust. Armor does not protect.

- **Weakness (Holy Symbol):** A character with a holy symbol may keep a vampire at bay by displaying a holy symbol. A vampire who wants to directly attack the victim must beat her in an opposed test of Spirits.
- **Weakness (Holy Water):** A vampire sprinkled with holy water is Fatigued. If immersed, he combusts as if it were direct sunlight (see above).
- **Weakness (Invitation Only):** Vampires cannot enter a private dwelling without being invited. They may enter public domains as they please.
- **Weakness (Stake Through the Heart):** A vampire hit with a called shot to the heart (−4) must make a Vigor roll versus the damage. If successful, it takes damage normally. If it fails, it disintegrates to dust.

VAMPIRE, YOUNG

Blood-drinkers of lore are common in many fantasy games. This is a relatively young vampire minion.

Attributes: Agility d8, Smarts d8, Spirit d8, Strength d12+1, Vigor d10

WEREWOLF

When a full moon emerges, humans infected with lycanthropy lose control and become snarling creatures bent on murder. Some embrace their cursed state and revel in the destruction they cause.

Attributes: Agility d8, Smarts d6, Spirit d6, Strength d12+2, Vigor d10

Skills: Climb d8, Fighting d12+2, Guts d10, Intimidation d10, Notice d12, Swimming d10, Stealth d10, Tracking d10

Pace: 8; **Parry:** 9; **Toughness:** 7

Special Abilities

- **Claws:** Str+d8.
- **Fear −2:** Werewolves chill the blood of all who see them.
- **Infection:** Anyone slain by a werewolf has a 50% chance of rising as a werewolf themselves. The character involuntarily transforms every full moon. He gains control of his lycanthropy only after 1d6 years as a werewolf.
- **Invulnerability:** Werewolves can only be Shaken by weapons that are not silver—not wounded.
- **Infravision:** Werewolves can see heat and halve penalties for bad lighting when attacking living targets.
- **Weakness:** Werewolves suffer normal damage from silver weapons.

ZOMBIE

These walking dead are typical groaning fiends looking for fresh meat.

Attributes: Agility d6, Smarts d4, Spirit d4, Strength d6, Vigor d6

Skills: Fighting d6, Intimidation d6, Notice d4, Shooting d6

Pace: 4; **Parry:** 5; **Toughness:** 7

Special Abilities

- **Claws:** Str.
- **Fearless:** Zombies are immune to Fear and Intimidation.
- **Undead:** +2 Toughness. +2 to recover from being Shaken. Called shots do no extra damage (except to the head).
- **Weakness (Head):** Shots to a zombie's head are +2 damage.

The Wreck of the Solarah
A Piratical Savage Tale for Novice Characters

The time is the Golden Age of Piracy, sometime in the early late 1600s. The player characters are a crew with a small sloop looking to make their fortune in the Caribbean. Whether they are pirates, privateers, or simple merchantmen with a lag in contracts is up to them, but all are Novice characters looking for adventure.

The tale starts at the port of Nassau, in a tavern called *The Last Resort*. A fellow by the name of Pete, a former pirate by the look of him, is deep in his cups and claims to know the location of a lost treasure ship called the *Solarah*.

For a fee—say the starting wages of a single character (typically $500)—Pete reveals the location. Threats might also work, but the rest of the scoundrels in *The Last Resort* won't look kindly to one of their own being bullied right before their noses.

The Map

Pete claims he and his pirate mates chased the Solarah to ground on an island roughly three days west of Tortuga. The crew decided to fight from land, but as the buccaneers watched the Spanish were attacked by savage cannibals and carted off to some horrid fate on the cliffs above.

Pete quietly produces a map that any sailor worth his salt can follow and returns to his drunken ramblings.

The Journey

The journey can be as short or epic as you choose. Perhaps the adventurers encounter pirates, or turn pirate themselves. Or perhaps they must sail through fierce storms or evade privateers.

When their journey is finally over, they find themselves on the shores of a small, crescent-shaped island roughly three miles long and a half-mile thick at its center.

The *Solarah* can be seen careened on the beach, mostly intact. There are several cannon-ball holes in her hull, but none larger than a man's fist (providing eerie light to the inside later on). Exploring the ship requires climbing up the tattered rigging or anchor chain to the main deck. This is a simple Climbing roll, with failure resulting in Fatigue caused by bumps and bruises.

The Wreck

The ship was a galleon fully-loaded with treasure. The local cannibals have taken most everything of any useful value, including several chests of gold and silver. A few scattered remnants (Notice roll to find 1d6 doubloons per character) remain, however, proving that such a treasure did exist.

Exploring the wreck is a creepy affair as several skeletons lie among the ruins. A Common Knowledge roll reveals they were likely slain before the ship beached, most likely by cannon shot or the resulting splinters.

Furniture, hammocks, and other goods

have mostly been ripped out. All the food has been taken as well, though the character who rolls the highest Notice finds a small but intact cask of rum beneath some debris.

The captain's cabin reveals a surprise— scattered bits and pieces of wardrobe and makeup reveal a woman was on board the Solarah. A Common Knowledge roll hints that she may still be alive—the cannibals of these islands often keep captured females as slave-queens!

The Slave-Queen!

It isn't hard to find the cannibals who rule this small isle—they live on a mountain in the center around a deep pool that feeds a dramatic, 40' high waterfall. Heroic characters might want to follow the obvious trails to the village, making Stealth rolls to slip past occasional guards (and quickly subduing or fighting those they alert).

At the top of the mountain are a couple of dozen grass huts lined up along the pool toward the waterfall. Between some of the grass huts are campfires with spits or crude clay pots (and one metal one taken from the ship). Bones lie everywhere—both animal and otherwise. It should be immediately obvious the natives are cannibals.

One hut seems larger than the rest. This is the home of the Chief, who has indeed taken the Spanish maiden Isabella from the Solarah as his bride. The slave-queen is set to consummate her marriage on the blood-moon—the very night the heroes arrive! This should be eventually obvious from watching the preparations at the village and Isabella's sobs. They should also see the cannibals' offerings to the Gods—piles of gold and silver thrown into the near-infinite depths of the pool (in reality a massively deep "blue hole").

It's now up to the heroes to save Isabella and recover the treasure. How they do this is entirely up to them. There are 30 cannibals of

fighting age in and around the village. They are deadly as a group, but could be distracted or drawn off by a clever plan.

Isabella is a human with d6 in all stats and the Very Attractive Edge. Who she is and why she was on a Spanish treasure ship is up to you, but it should certainly lead to more adventure, and more Savage Tales!

CANNIBALS

The cannibals are pure stereotypes. Describe them as nasty, dirty savages with black, jagged teeth and strange piercings and tattoos. The women and children vanish into the jungle at the first sign of trouble leaving only warriors behind. One out of ever 10 cannibals is a war leader—a Wild Card.
Attributes: Agility d6, Smarts d4, Spirit d6, Strength d8, Vigor d8
Skills: Fighting d8, Guts d6, Intimidation d8, Notice d6, Stealth d8, Throwing d6
Pace: 6; **Parry:** 7; **Toughness:** 6
Gear: Spear (Reach 1; Str+d6; Parry +1)

GET SAVAGE!

SETTINGS!

The **Savage Worlds** "Fast! Furious! Fun!" design philosophy can be found in our setting books as well. Most of our worlds are "Plot Point" books designed to give you the structure of a scripted backstory with the openness of a traditional campaign. Run the game straight "out of the box" or add your own adventures as you see fit!

COMMUNITY!

The **Savage Worlds** community is one of the most active and friendly places on the net! Ask rule questions, find conversions for your favorite games or movies, talk to the designers, and meet local players on our forums!

SAVAGE TALES!

Pinnacle constantly publishes new Savage Tales, adventures for all our settings as well as brand new worlds as e-books on our website. From our popular One Sheets™ to fully fleshed-out adventures, you'll find no end of excitement for you and your friends!

OUR NEWEST SAVAGE WORLDS

LOOKING FOR TEMPLATES, CHARACTER SHEETS, AND FREE ADVENTURES? GO TO OUR WEBSITE AT WWW.PEGINC.COM!